Comments

What People Are Saying About Al Parinello and *On The Air*

"It's real simple: If you aspire to become a sought-after radio and TV talk-show guest, you *must* read Al Parinello's book. He leaves nothing to the imagination; every detail is clearly revealed. No other source exists for getting this kind of insider information in concise, easy-to-understand form."

Robert Ringer,
Author of
Winning Through Intimidation

On
The Air

How To Get On
Radio And TV Talk Shows
And What To Do
When You Get There

By Al Parinello

THE CAREER PRESS
180 FIFTH AVENUE
PO BOX 34
HAWTHORNE, NJ 07507
1-800-CAREER 1
201-427-0229 (OUTSIDE U.S.)
FAX: 201-427-2037

On The Air: How To Get On Radio and TV Talk Shows And What To Do When You Get There

ISBN 0-934829-85-3, $12.95

Cover design by Dean Johnson Design, Inc.

Copies of this volume may be ordered by mail or phone directly from the publisher. To order by mail, please include price as noted above, $2.50 handling per order, as well as $1.00 for each book ordered. Send to: The Career Press, Inc., 180 Fifth Ave., P.O. Box 34, Hawthorne, N.J. 07507

Or call Toll-free 1-800-CAREER-1 (in Canada: 201-427-0229) to order using your VISA or MasterCard or for further information on all books published or distributed by The Career Press.

For Anita and Dana,

the ladies in my life

Contents

On
The Air

Acknowledgements

The Cast
Of the Show

Creating, researching, writing and publishing a book is by no means a lonely job. The cast of contributors is large, even though only one gets the coveted author credit. This author wishes to thank the many personal and professional friends and associates who so graciously gave their time and expertise.

First and foremost, I'd like to thank my wife, Anita, who has given me her time, support and the use of her left brain. My brilliant publisher, Ron Fry, whose philosophy is "Get the job done, but only if it's fun." My logical and perceptive editor, Betsy Sheldon, who, I'm convinced, knows more about the media than I do. My partner and co-host of *"Your Own Success,"* Jay Campbell, who affably sat in the shadows and supported my efforts with his wisdom. And Judy Smith, whose computer talents are unparalleled.

When I asked for help from the many celebrities, personalities and friends who have appeared on my own syndicated talk show, I was deluged with responses. My special thanks to Ken Blanchard, Skip Cypert, Bert Decker, Tom Peters, Carole Hyatt, Orson Bean, Og Mandino, Dr. Lane Longfellow, Barbara Abrams Mintzer, Fred Pryor, Art Linkletter, Shari Lewis, Barbara Brabec, Robert Half, Michael LeBoeuf, Jimmy Calano, Dr. Peter Hanson, Jim

Cathcart, Stew Leonard, Dottie Walters, Elysa Lazar, Austin McGonigle, Richard Lederer, Warren Bennis, Dr. Stephen Covey, Don Richard Riso, Dr. Vernon Mark, Roy Grutman, Jonathan Evetts, Ted Dreier, Stan Katz, Jeanette Reddish Scollard, Harry Lorayne, David Gumpert, Ron Rotstein, Mikki Williams, Dr. Gilda Carle, Jane and Robert Handly, Warren Greshes, Roger Herman, Robert Ringer, Roger Dawson, Dorothy Leeds, Peter Glen, John Diebold, Allan Cox, Gil Eagles, Bob Hochheiser, Joe Mancuso, Dr. Wayne Dyer, David Brown and Al Neuharth.

Thank you, also, to those who responded but whose contributions, because of unavoidable circumstances, could not be included, a fact that does not in any way diminish my gratitude.

This book would not have been conceived, nor would there have been a talk show industry about which to write, if not for the efforts of Steve Allen and Barry Gray. Today's television talk shows still employ most of the components introduced decades earlier by Mr. Allen, the creator of *"The Tonight Show."* The same can be said of radio call-in talk shows, which Mr. Gray is credited with originating. I am honored to have met and worked with both of these industry giants. Both are gentle and selfless, and both have contributed more than they can possibly know to this book and to my own success.

Introduction

Yes, There's A Place For *You* On The Air!

Dedicated talk radio fan Eugene Steichen was listening to Minneapolis radio station KQRS's "Dead or Not Dead" trivia show when he realized he knew the answers to the show's questions. He quickly called in, got through and answered, correctly, that Orson Bean and Polly Bergen were alive, but Norm Van Brocklin, Bob Montana and Leadbelly were dead. Steichen's good fortune was short-lived. Another listener recognized his voice and immediately called the police.

Steichen— who had escaped from a Minnesota prison just a few months earlier— found a unique way to be recaptured.

Never underestimate the power of the electronic media.

Andy Warhol once predicted that in the future everyone would be famous for 15 minutes. The future is rapidly becoming the present. The far-reaching powers of the electronic media can indeed enable any of us to enjoy a few moments of celebrity status, becoming familiar to stockbrokers on Wall Street, steel workers in Gary, retirees in Sun City, the movers and shakers on the West Coast— or the prison authorities in Minnesota.

But this book isn't about how to achieve 15 minutes of fame. The unfortunate Mr. Steichen is better qualified to write that kind of book than me. This is a book that reveals to you the power of the media, that identifies the opportunity provided by the more than 1,000 TV and radio talk shows on the air in the United States and Canada today. Collectively, these shows require more than 20,000 guests every week. *That's more than 1 million qualified guests in demand each year–* and *you* should be one of them.

You're *not* a celebrity? So what?

I'm going to assume a few things about you: You aren't up for an Oscar nomination this year. You haven't recently discovered a cure for AIDS. You're not a key player in the most current political scandal. And I certainly hope you haven't been the victim of domestic violence.

More likely, you're an entrepreneur who's built your own business and is looking for new ways to attract customers. Or you're a writer trying to spread the word about your new book. Maybe you're a professional speaker or a seminar leader who wants to reach more audiences. Or an inspired environmental activist, dedicated to converting the public to a greater consciousness.

In other words, although your story may never appear on the front page of any of the tabloids prominently displayed at the checkout counter, you *do* have something to say! And sharing your news on television or radio will definitely benefit you in some way. You're not merely looking for 15 minutes of fame. You're hoping to increase your business, boost the sales of your book, attract more attendees to your seminar or class, or incite more involvement in your cause.

Is there a guest chair with *your* name on it?

You don't have to be a celebrity, a controversial politician or a criminal to appear on a television or radio talk show. Entertaining and interesting guests like you are in high demand by the more than 1,000 talk shows broadcast each week, every day, throughout North America. Believe me, I know! As creator, co-host and executive producer of the nationally syndicated radio program, *"Your Own Success,"* I've invited more than 2,500 guests– from celebrities to cab drivers– to sit in the guest chair. Through my experience with *"Your Own Success"* and a host of other TV and radio talk shows, I've discovered just how valuable interesting guests are.

And I've discovered something even more incredible: Less than five percent of the guests I've interviewed are truly prepared to take full advantage of the wonderful opportunity to market themselves to the largest and most responsive audience that they'll ever reach. While most talk show guests give great interviews, they still blow it. They miss their chance to shine in the spotlight, to turn their appearance into a successful promotion that reaps them future benefits. Why? I can only imagine they do so because they don't know *how* to take advantage of the talk show opportunity.

By reading this book, and following the course of action it sets forth, you'll discover how to *land* a talk show interview, what to do once you *get* there to maximize the result of your appearance, and what to do *afterward* to garner even more exposure.

But first, let's examine why and how talk show interviews can be a valuable part of your marketing plan– whether you want to promote your product, your service, your cause or yourself.

The must-do interview: WII-F M

WII-FM. The most important call letters for anyone pursuing an appearance on radio or TV. If you can remember them, your appearances on talk shows will pay off handsomely.

WII-FM stands for "What's In It For Me?" And it's a question you should make sure you've answered carefully before you proceed with any interview.

In my position of interviewing thousands of guests, I can see that not many are familiar with the reach and impact of WII-FM. This is a shame, because WII-FM can do a lot to give every talk show guest the positive exposure that they seek.

Keep WII-FM in mind when you're seeking an appearance, when you've been invited to interview on a talk show, when you're preparing for your interview, even while you're sitting in the guest chair.

What's in it for you?

A chance to tell thousands of people about your business? An opportunity to promote your upcoming seminar? Get some exposure for your book? Get people backing your cause? Sending donations? Buying your product?

Always make the interview work for you. If you keep this in mind, WII-FM will be working for you from now on, no matter what station you appear on.

The dollars and sense of the interview

A one-minute advertising spot can cost as much as $1,000 on a major-market radio station. On local television, a 30-second spot can cost more than $10,000. But your appearance as a guest on a talk show costs you *nothing*. Yet your 10-minute local TV interview might be worth as much as $200,000!

Editorial minutes are as valuable as advertising minutes, if not more so. Some radio listeners tune out commercial messages, leave the room (if they're not in a car), or switch to a different station. TV viewers are known to accomplish important tasks during commercials, like visiting the bathroom or getting a snack. Remote control units have made "zapping" commercials almost as popular as popcorn at the movies!

Furthermore, audiences often perceive the editorial portion as more credible. Most viewers and listeners recognize that commercials are providing biased, one-sided information solely to convince them to spend money on something. On the other hand, audiences tend to perceive the editorial portion of programming as a more objective dissemination of information– even if it's saying the same thing or touting the same product. While the statement, "Most doctors recommend Brand X" may or may not be true, it's likely that more people will believe this statement if presented in an editorial format rather than within an advertisement.

Through your talk show appearance, you are reaching the same receptive audience that advertisers pay thousands to reach– and you may have more impact than the commercials. So even though you're not paying for your appearance, treat it as the invaluable opportunity it is.

In the chapters to follow, I'll suggest how you can take full advantage of the experience of being a guest on a radio or TV program. Specifically, we'll discuss the "how to's" of getting on talk shows, the best behaviors for the various types of talk shows, and, more importantly, how to get something out of the experience, over and above a few minutes of fame. Lastly, we'll discuss the importance of getting invited back and how to better your chances. Along the way, we'll meet an eclectic group of people who have all struggled along these paths before and have valuable things to say about their experiences– insights that can save you time, money and embarrassment.

Whether you're a small business entrepreneur, community activist, author, professional speaker, salesperson, travel agent, educator, health specialist or cab driver, you can harness the power of radio and TV talk shows to achieve your goals. You can communicate with entire communities and in the process, market yourself and your products, services and points of view, free of charge, to an audience waiting to hear your story.

You don't have to be today's hot starlet, president of a $10 billion company or the originator of the latest fad to be in demand. All you have to be is an interesting man or woman with something to say. If that describes you, what are you waiting for?

Guesting on radio and television talk shows represents the great untapped marketing tool of the '90s. Tap into it and whether you appear for five minutes or 15, you'll gain immeasurable value– on the air.

Chapter 1

Do You Have 'Good Guest' Qualities?

Larry King, who has interviewed more than 30,000 people in his 30 years of experience, had this to say in his 1988 bestseller, *Tell it to the King*:

"There are certain qualities that make for a good guest. If the guest has them, it doesn't matter if he or she is a ballet dancer, plumber, politician, photographer, or songwriter, the show will be a good one.

"The first quality is an ability to explain to the layperson what they do. The second is a passion for what they do. Then they need a sense of humor, preferably one that's self-deprecating as well, and a little bit of a chip on their shoulder, a little anger. If they've got all four of those, you've got a great guest, regardless of the subject. If I get three out of four, I can usually have a good show."

Larry's right. The ability to communicate what you do—in a concise and entertaining way– is key to your success as an interview guest. I was recently buttonholed at a social event by a woman who wanted to be a guest on our show. After boring me for 10 minutes or so with uninteresting and unconnected information about how she helps people with their businesses or something like that, I interrupted her to ask, "What is it you do? And what is it you will talk about if you are a guest on the show?" She continued to ramble as I made a mental note never to invite her to guest.

Keep it short– or just keep it!

My own rule of thumb is, you should be able to say what you do in one sentence, using one- or two-syllable words. For example, "I help people make lots of money." In other words, if you can't write it on the back of your business card, it's too long!

Passion, humor and anger, as Larry attests, add the sizzle to your presentation. You want to convince the audience that you are the *most* qualified, *most* effective and *only* purveyor of your particular service that they would ever want to contact. Having a chip on your shoulder makes you interesting. If, for instance, you're an accountant, your appearance might be more effective if you express your anger at all the opportunities for tax savings that are blatantly ignored by taxpayers each year.

One of the best guests we've ever interviewed was David Liederman, who created the phenomenon known as David's Cookies, in New York City. He chose to talk about the effects of increasing crime on entrepreneurs and their retail businesses. He was mad because his stores had been robbed at gunpoint; he was angry at the police, the mayor, the drug problem. He probably got more listeners to buy his cookies by *not* talking about them, but about the plight of the retail entrepreneur.

So once again, clarify what it is that you do, and speak with passion, humor or– yes– even anger.

You don't have to be a star, baby

You need not be at the top of your profession– or even in a glamorous profession– to do well as a guest. You just need to be interesting.

I once invited a cab driver, an aspiring author, to appear on the program. All day, every day, he listened to the city's problems– all the things people wanted to say to their bosses, boyfriends, girlfriends, husbands and wives but couldn't find the guts to. He began writing notes at red lights and in heavy traffic. He called his unpublished book "How to be Happy" I booked him for what I thought would be a 10-minute interview. One *hour* and 10 minutes later, we said goodbye with the phones still ringing. I don't know what happened to him, but I do know that we received two calls from literary agents after the program was over.

Keep in mind that what makes a great guest for the *show* is different from what makes a great guest for the *guest*. You become a great guest when your appearance causes a response, specifically one that generates sales, increases your business, attracts new clients and increases your awareness in the marketplace. (In Chapters 4 and 5, you'll learn more about how to create such a response.)

With more than 2,500 notches on my interview belt, I've had plenty of experience with great, not-so-great, and just plain awful guests. And I've discovered that there are some categories of professions that make better guests than others. There are exceptions to every rule, of course, but I think the majority of my fellow talk show hosts would agree with the following broad categorization of top guests and "challenging" guests (which excludes performers, actors and other "professional" guests, both popular and notorious).

Best guests

- **Entrepreneurs:** Perky and self-assured. They come across as honest and hardworking people who really want to help the rest of us.

- **Authors:** Because they are so involved in their work, their information is fresh, interesting, and related with ease, confidence and the passion we discussed earlier.

- **Winners (Recipients) of Awards:** They usually communicate as humble and thankful people who really care about their cause.

- **Heroes/Humanitarians:** These human-interest stories always work well on TV or radio. Audiences seem to need heroes to worship. They can do no wrong in the eyes of the viewers and listeners.

- **Psychologists/Psychiatrists:** Because they focus on the how and why of the way we think and act, they provide interesting and thought-provoking interviews and stimulate audience involvement.

- **Psychics, Mentalists, Hypnotists, and Memory Experts:** I have a theory about these fascinating people. I believe they represent "hope without obligation." Everyone wants to know that something special and something more is available to them. These people represent that "something." Telephones will ring off the hook every time a guest in this category appears.

- **Motivational Speakers:** Everyone needs a pat on the back and a kick in the rear. This group challenges audiences to grow and to accomplish more. They are usually highly excitable and have great energy to share with viewers and listeners. They represent the hope we are all seeking.

- **Humorists:** We all want to laugh. A light conversation goes a long way on a TV or radio show. There is a reason that professional speakers are often told, "You don't *have* to be funny– only if you want to be invited back."

- **Eccentrics:** There will always be room on TV and radio talk shows for the person who communicates with space people, or the inventor who has finally discovered a better mouse trap. We have a fascination with other people's weird views and ideas.

The fact that you happen to fit into one of the preceding best-guest categories doesn't assure that you'll be welcomed with open arms. You still need to be interesting and have a point of view that is appealing to the producer.

'Challenging' guests

- **Accountants:** They tend to take an innately boring approach to an already dry topic, and usually pop up at tax time and just before January 1st (Tax Saving Time). Even the "Funniest Accountant in America" winner was dull!

- **Lawyers:** These guests are fearful of saying anything without consulting a legal source. They seem to fear that their interview will haunt them at a future date.

- **Corporate Executives:** Mostly these guests appear to be afraid of their own shadows. They only seem comfortable speaking "the corporate line," the one approved by company attorneys.

- **Financial Experts:** As a rule, the downfall of these numbers-oriented guests is their tendency to talk like human computers. They risk appearing cold and– most dangerous of all– smarter than the rest of us.

- **Computer Professionals:** See above (Financial Experts).

- **Sports Celebrities:** One-act plays. After you say "it," there's usually nothing left to say. "That

was a great game on Sunday, Bubba." "Thanks, I
played hard." Sports figures make great guests
for sports shows only, and then for only three
minutes.

- **Politicians:** Usually, they have an agenda in
  mind and they won't move from it. They have the
  capacity to drone on and on and still look
  interested.

- **Medical Professionals:** After the first few
  minutes, they tend to revert to "medical-ese,"
  speaking above the average audience (and the
  average talk show host).

- **Career Counselors:** The word boring comes to
  mind, but not because their message is boring,
  it's just always the same: "Try harder, keep your
  nose to the grindstone, write a good resume,
  here's how to ask for a raise in a nice way, and
  don't date your boss's daughter." *Ho hum.*

- **Speakers, Trainers and Seminar Leaders:**
  Surprised? Because they are accustomed to being
  in charge, these guests sometimes have difficulty
  handling the number-two spot in an interview.
  Also, they may have timing problems with the
  electronic media. They are accustomed to
  building stories and examples slowly into
  climactic endings. They can't seem to pace themselves as effectively on radio or television.

- **Members of Civic Groups:** They would be
  advised to explore a unique angle or go into
  depth about their group's intentions, growth, etc.
  Generally, after they tell the audience about next
  Tuesday's bake-off, it's all over.

- **New Age Representatives:** "Okay, now, everybody get out your crystals, cross your legs, hum in unison and everything will be much better." I have not found anyone yet who will tell us why we should do these things, beyond that "it feels good." How about some data, sources, and solid research (but not from India)?

Remember: All talk show hosts have stories galore about guests who were *supposed* to be great, and tales of guests they dreaded– and have appeared 12 times since! So don't feel too cocky if your profession makes you a "great guest." And if your profession is listed in the "challenger" category, maybe *knowing* that will give you the drive to become a great guest anyway.

Chapter 2

Where To Begin: Do Your Homework

You've determined that you do indeed have what it takes to be an entertaining talk show guest, and that your appearance on a TV or radio talk show will give your product, service, business or yourself the exposure you want.

You're starting to write down pithy stories and save up amusing anecdotes. You're budgeting for new clothes, even a new hairstyle. You're ready to trade quips with Johnny and intellectualize with Ted Koppel.

Now what?

Research the media

Your first step is to learn as much as you can about your options. In other words, what television and radio shows are out there? Which appeal to the audiences you most want to reach? And which are more likely to invite you to be a guest?

The best place to begin your search is in your own living room. Just turn on the TV or radio, and spend a few hours watching and listening. Most radio talk programs are categorized as *general talk* or *news talk*. Unless you're a political strategist or politician, you'll probably only be interested in general talk– programs on just about any subject from pets to world travel.

As you seek out general talk programs, don't eliminate opportunities prematurely. For example, some radio stations program music during the day and talk only in the evenings or on weekends. Listen at the wrong time and you may wrongly conclude a station isn't for you. So tune in at different *times* of the day and on different *days*. Check your local newspaper for TV and radio listings. And don't hesitate to contact the stations directly for a programming schedule.

Most local TV stations produce some of their own programming. Much of this is public-service programming, but there may be other local news and entertainment shows that provide excellent interview opportunities. You should zap through all your local channels in early morning (5:30 to 10 a.m.), late afternoon (3 to 6 p.m.), and late night (midnight to 3 a.m.) to find these sometimes hidden gems.

About radio talk shows

As you investigate your radio opportunities, you should realize that most talk formats will be on the AM (Amplitude Modulation) band width. Music formats dominate FM (Frequency Modulation), because of its higher-quality stereo sound. FM has the vast majority of radio's listening audience (about 75 percent), but don't assume that AM stations are weaker, or that no one listens to AM.

AM listeners tend to be more mature and better educated– and that just may be the audience you want to reach. AM stations in the major cities continue to remain dominant in ratings, year after year, over their FM competitors.

There are two blocks of time every weekday when radio listenership is appreciably higher than all other times.

"Drive time" consists of the hours from 6 a.m. to 10 a.m. and 3 p.m. to 7 p.m— when most employed people are either going to or coming home from work. (The term "drive time" was coined by the late radio pioneer Gerard Bartell, who discovered that listener dedication during specific times could earn premium advertising dollars for those blocks. His Wisconsin radio stations were the first to capitalize on this phenomenon.) You should try at all costs to be a guest on as many radio programs during these peak times as you can.

One note of caution about drive time: Because most listeners *are* driving, they can't readily (and safely) scribble down your address or other lengthy information. An easy-to-remember "800" or local telephone number is your best solution to this problem. When I appear on talk shows to publicize this book, it's a joy to give out the number for my publisher, Career Press: 1-800-CAREER-1. How can you forget a number like that?

You can call the telephone company to arrange for your own catchy number. They are surprisingly inexpensive given their unparalleled advantages. Just remember: The easier they are to remember, the greater your response will probably be.

My favorite so far has got to be 1-800-Mattress. (Don't ask!)

Your best markets: The bigger, the better

As you expand your exploration of talk radio and TV beyond your own area, you should become aware of and appreciate the importance of market size. The following chart lists the top 100 broadcast markets and indicates the total population in those areas— that is, how many potential viewers and listeners there are. Note that the top 25 markets represent about 50 percent of the population of the United States. About 25 percent reside in the top six markets alone.

Top 100 Broadcast Markets

(Based on 1980 Census, updated to Jan. 1, 1990. Population figures are based on age 12 and up, rounded to the nearest thousand.)

Rank	Market	Population
1	New York, NY	17,274,000
2	Los Angeles, CA	12,528,000
3	Chicago, IL	9,858,000
4	San Francisco, CA	8,305,000
5	Philadelphia, PA	7,218,000
6	Boston, MA	6,046,000
7	Detroit, MI	5,255,000
8	Dallas/Ft Worth, TX	4,800,000
9	Washington, DC	4,547,000
10	Houston, TX	3,736,000
11	Miami, FL	3,655,000
12	Pittsburgh, PA	3,470,000
13	San Jose, CA	3,345,000
14	Cleveland, OH	3,339,000
15	Atlanta, GA	3,252,000
16	Minneapolis, MN	3,157,000
17	St. Louis, MO	3,021,000
18	Seattle/Tacoma, WA	2,830,000
19	Tampa, FL	2,824,000
20	Baltimore, MD	2,703,000
21	Sacramento, CA	2,589,000
22	Hartford, CT	2,540,000
23	Denver, CO	2,502,000
24	Phoenix, AZ	2,313,000
25	Kansas City, KS	2,300,000
26	Nassau/Suffolk, NY	2,245,000
27	Orlando, FL	2,192,000

28	Indianapolis, IN	2,123,000
29	Providence, RI	2,101,000
30	W. Palm Beach, FL	2,087,000
31	San Diego, CA	2,047,000
32	Charlotte, NC	1,976,000
33	Anaheim/Santa Ana, CA	1,936,000
34	New Orleans, LA	1,896,000
35	Columbus, OH	1,892,000
36	Cincinnati, OH	1,885,000
37	Greensboro/High Point/ Winston-Salem, NC	1,872,000
38	Raleigh/Durham, NC	1,869,000
39	Milwaukee/Racine, WI	1,825,000
40	Portland, OR	1,765,000
41	Riverside/San Bernardino, CA	1,727,000
42	San Antonio, TX	1,721,000
43	Birmingham, AL	1,705,000
44	Memphis, TN	1,659,000
45	Nashville, TN	1,651,000
46	Norfolk/Virginia Beach, VA	1,634,000
47	Dayton, OH	1,537,000
48	Albany/Schenectady/Troy, NY	1,448,000
49	Oklahoma City, OK	1,423,000
50	Salt Lake City, UT	1,400,000
51	Harrisburg/Lebanon, PA	1,400,000
52	Buffalo/Niagara Falls, NY	1,399,000
53	Greenville/Spartanburg, NC	1,375,000
54	Grand Rapids, MI	1,318,000
55	Louisville, KY	1,291,000
56	Knoxville, TN	1,263,000
57	Tulsa, OK	1,243,000
58	York, PA	1,233,000
59	Rochester, NY	1,169,000
60	Omaha, NB	1,166,000
61	Baton Rouge, LA	1,165,000
62	New Haven, CT	1,128,000
63	Wilkes Barre/Scranton, PA	1,120,000

64	Little Rock, AR	1,083,000
65	Saginaw,Bay City, WI	1,064,000
66	Roanoke/Lynchburg, WV	1,064,000
67	Akron, OH	1,052,000
68	Toledo, OH	1,043,000
69	Fresno, CA	1,042,000
70	Jacksonville, FL	1,035,000
71	Richmond, VA	1,019,000
72	Syracuse, NY	1,007,000
73	Des Moines, IA	991,000
74	Austin, TX	972,000
75	Albuquerque, NM	930,000
76	Mobile, AL	921,000
77	Shreveport, LA	920,000
78	Modesto, CA	900,000
79	Coastal, NC	899,000
80	Allentown/Bethlehem, PA	889,000
81	Jackson, MS	883,000
82	Lansing, MI	864,000
83	Fort Wayne, IN	842,000
84	Lexington, KY	841,000
85	Monmouth/Ocean, NJ	839,000
86	Youngstown, OH	822,000
87	Madison, WI	799,000
88	Santa Barbara, CA	794,000
89	Chattanooga, TN	777,000
90	Huntsville, AL	775,000
91	Columbia, SC	767,000
92	South Bend, IN	767,000
93	Green Bay, WI	767,000
94	Tucson, AZ	744,000
95	Charleston, SC	736,000
96	Melbourne/Titusville, FL	734,000
97	Spokane, WA	726,000
98	Johnson City/Bristol, TN	722,000
99	Charleston, WV	719,000
100	Lancaster, PA	714,000

How to learn about talk shows nationwide

Updated lists of radio and television stations are available from various sources, including mailing-list companies you'll find listed in the yellow pages, or the **Annual Broadcasting Yearbook,** which you can purchase for $115 (Broadcasting Yearbook, 1705 DeSales Street N.W., Washington, D. C. 20036).

For a current list of all stations and networks known to carry talk-formatted shows, be sure to refer to the comprehensive Databanks at the back of this book— its pages include the top nationally syndicated radio and TV talk show programs, a market-by-market breakdown of talk-formatted radio stations, and a top 100 market breakdown for TV stations, throughout the U.S. and Canada. Use the Databanks to determine which stations to contact to find out more about specific talk show programs that may promise opportunity for you. All listings include addresses, telephone contact numbers and fax numbers, if available.

This information will offer you a good start in your research. But, if you're ready to find out exactly which local stations have viable talk shows for you, you'll want a more targeted list, with names of producers. If you have contacts in the public relations industry, you can ask if they can hunt down such information. *Or* you can contact me at American Media Ventures, P.O. Box 279, Norwood, N.J. 07648, (201) 784-0059. As a media consultant, I am always aware of the best and cleanest list for use by my clients.

Four outside interview sources

As you prepare to publicize yourself, your product, service or cause to attract talk show interest, there are some sources available to help you. In this industry, printed sources come and go rapidly, so I've decided to list the four that I believe are the absolute best, those that have proven themselves over time.

1. *Radio - TV Interview Report Magazine*

This bimonthly magazine was launched four years ago and is currently distributed free to 4,700 talk show producers and hosts. Each 72-page issue features profiles on about 100 would-be guests who have each paid between $45 and $727 for the privilege of reaching these decision-makers. Discounts are available for multiple-issue advertising.

Glancing through a current issue, I was stopped by ad headlines such as: "Should children with AIDS be allowed in public schools?," "Train your intuition to work for you," "Can you be ethical and still make money?," "How to quit smoking," "Is the diet industry a fraud?" and "You can cut hair!"

The magazine is published by Bradley Communications Corp. (135 East Plumstead Avenue, Lansdowne, Pa. 19050-1206; 215-259-1070).

2. *The Yearbook of Experts, Authorities, and Spokespersons*

This 800-page annual directory is delivered to more than 7,000 of the country's top working journalists. For a $225 fee, you can include a 50-word advertisement in the publication and a nine-key word listing in the index section. The most recent edition has listings for organizations and individuals as diverse as: Inventors Workshop International, California's Expert on Government Red Tape, Coalition to End the Permanent Congress, National Flag Foundation, Seamless Garment Network, Gun Owners of America, Smokers' Rights Alliance, Prison Fellowship Ministries, National Victim Center, and Professor Yo-Yo, who bills himself as the only Yo-Yo in Washington who knows what he's doing.

For information about placement, contact Mitchell Davis, editor, at the Broadcast Interview Source (2500 Wisconsin Ave NW Suite 930, Washington, D. C. 20007-4570; 202-333-4904; Fax 202-342-5411).

3. *Newsmaker Interviews*

This eight-year-old monthly newsletter reaches 150 radio stations and national television shows every month. The good news about this publication that reaches a small but mighty readership is that it doesn't cost *you*– the talk show guest– anything for a listing. The bad news is that it's very difficult to get a listing.

Subscribers pay between $480 to $960 a year to read 200-word bios about 47 newsmakers each month. According to editor Arthur Levine, criteria for listing include: unusualness of subject, offbeat ideas, national flavor, and celebrity status. Some recent issues offered these stories:

Harry and Wally's Favorite TV Shows"
"The 1990's: The Grey Decade– The Aging of America"
"Timothy Leary Flashes Back on His Own Life"
"Skitch Henderson and Wife Ruth Share Cooking Secrets"
"Teaching, How to Heal Through Laughter"
"Analyzing Your Own Dreams Can Change Your Life"

If you believe you meet the criteria for a listing, contact *Newsmaker Interviews* (8217 Beverly Blvd., Los Angeles, Calif. 90048; 213-655-2793; Fax 213-275-2602).

4. *Party Line*

In the other publications listed in this chapter, you as the prospective talk show guest place the ad or listing and wait to be contacted by the talk show producer. *Party Line,* a 30-year-old weekly publication, works differently.

When producers decide to do a story and seek guests to interview, they contact *Party Line* to include a listing featuring their guest needs. Publicists and other subscribers can then scan the listings for opportunities for their clients or for themselves. You can subscribe to *Party Line,* which costs $145 a year, by contacting Betty Yarmon, editor (*Party Line* 35 Sutton Place, New York, N.Y. 10022; 212-755-3487; Fax 212-755-3488.)

A final word about cable TV

There is cable television, and there is *Cable Television*. This is an important distinction if you're considering seeking an interview on a cable talk show. Cable reaches, as of this writing, 60 million American homes. Yet, these subscribers are spread out among more than 10,000 systems, most of which are local and unconnected. While the largest systems may have 400,000 subscribers, there are few systems that large– many have as few as 100 subscribers.

America's television viewing habits favor the four major networks and independent stations over cable by a margin of three to one. That is, more than 65 percent of TV viewers still watch broadcasts over cablecasts.

Of cable channels, the basic satellite channels– such as CNN and MTV– attract most cable viewers, Next are the channels for which subscribers must pay an additional monthly fee– The Disney Channel, HBO and Showtime, for example. Last and abysmally least are the local channels, sometimes called public-access channels– rarely promoted, usually lost among popular fare. Very small audiences are tuning into most of the locally produced talk shows.

Even in large markets like New York City and Long Island, or San Diego and San Jose, the public-access channels are treated by management as a necessary evil. They *are* necessary so that the franchise requirements are met by the local cable TV system. Yet they tend to be poorly funded, mechanically inferior and ignored by management.

My advice is to guest on a locally produced cable TV program for experience alone, not exposure. And certainly not stardom!

Chapter 3

Getting
On The Air
The Right Way

You've completed your investigation of all the interview opportunities available to you– and identified which talk shows would be most advantageous or likely for you to appear on.

So how do you get on?

There are two ways, and both are devoid of mystery. You either contact the show or you're invited to appear. Of course, I've simplified the matter, but your chances of landing an appearance can only increase if you take the correct steps to get there. The more professional, sophisticated and savvy your presentation of yourself, the more likely you'll receive an invitation to guest. In order to impress the talk show producer who will determine whether you appear, you'd better do your homework.

Should you hire a publicist?

A publicist, a professional in the business of generating publicity for a company, an individual or an event, can do your leg work for you in terms of landing your guest appearances. Obviously, the advantages of working with an

experienced professional who has contacts and an understanding of the industry are numerous. Following are just a
few:

1. A good publicist will know the "inside story" on
   most of the talk shows you may be interested in.
   Your publicist should be able to advise you on
   which shows it would be most advantageous for
   you to appear– and which shows might actually
   be willing to book you.

2. Your publicist may already have contacts with
   many of the producers you'll wish to approach.
   Sometimes a phone call from a publicist can
   generate an interview on a station in a major
   market. A publicist knows *who* to call and, more
   importantly, *when* to call.

3. An effective publicist will take care of details you
   don't even know about. And he or she will be
   tenacious about following up.

4. A publicist is usually an experienced writer. This
   skill is important, whether he or she is writing
   letters to talk show producers or disseminating
   effective press releases to the media before your
   appearance.

5. Your publicist will advise you, once you've
   succeeded in getting an interview, on how to
   prepare, what to wear, and much more. He or
   she is trained to recognize your strengths and
   develop them, to know your weaknesses and help
   you downplay or avoid them.

6. A good publicist is able to see "the big picture,"
   keeping on top of all ongoing tasks involving
   your interview activity, and keeping in mind
   your future opportunities as well, which leaves
   you free to focus on your business.

Particularly if you're on a small budget, however, hiring a publicist is a decision that requires strong justification. Here are some points you should consider before hiring a publicist.

1. Monthly fees for a publicist range from $1,000 to $5,000 or more. In addition, you as the client are usually expected to cover normal business expenses, such as fax, mail or messenger services.

2. A publicist can only do something *with* something. If your only claim to fame is that you knot humorous potholders, don't expect much placement, even if you are paying on the high end.

3. If you are "hot," your publicist will keep you running from interview to interview– at a much more frantic pace than you might commit to on your own. The whirlwind will allow little time for anything else in your life (so be ready!).

Some publicists work on a per-placement basis or will take some clients on this basis– you pay if and only when you're scheduled to appear on a particular program, based on a predetermined rate schedule. There are both positive and negative aspects to this type of arrangement. The positive is obvious: You only pay after you receive a placement. The negative is that your account will usually be relegated to the least activity, your story pitched to producers as an afterthought, usually to the same producer who has just said "yes" to a monthly fee-paying client.

Your next step: Contacting the producer

If you decide to go it alone, your next step will be to talk to the show's producer, whose name you should know before you call. (If you don't, when you call the station and ask for the producer, be sure to get his or her name in case you're not able to get through the first time.) It's essential that you talk to the *producer; not* an administrative assistant, *not* a receptionist, not even the *host*. Why? Because it is the producer who will decide whether you will appear on the show.

(Because job changes can occur at a swift pace in television and radio production, when you establish contact with the producer, try to get the name of an assistant producer or another producer to use as a "standby." Go back to this person in the event your contact vanishes during the waiting period.)

During your phone call with the producer, you should be brief and to the point. Producers are usually very busy and (they'll tell you) very underpaid. Identify yourself, your intention, and offer some good reasons why you should be considered to guest on the show. *Don't* expect to "close the deal" in the first telephone call. If the producer is interested, he or she will probably ask you to send some information about yourself and your topic or tell you your material will be reviewed and someone will get back with you. Don't be disappointed– this means you are *still in the running,* even if you haven't gotten a commitment for a booking.

Following are a few other tips for a successful phone call to the producer:

- Never pretend to be your own publicist. If you are calling for yourself, state that fact. Don't slickly try to use a fake name when it's *you* you're representing.

- Don't try to overimpress. Don't lie. Don't exaggerate. Producers have developed a sixth sense– they can tell a phony, immediately. When phonies are discovered, the word gets around rapidly, and your talk-show future will abruptly end.

- If the answer is No, the answer is No! The producer knows who is listening to the show. Remember, he or she *is* looking for the right guest, but it very well may not be *you*. Don't take a rejection personally, just move on to your next source. If you get a "no" from the producer, don't make the mistake of asking if he or she can recommend another show in town. It's not in his or her best interest for a producer to act as your publicist. Nor does it make you seem too professional.

Your media kit: A valuable tool

Presuming you've managed to generate a little interest from a producer or three, your next step will be to mail your media kit– a packet of materials about you and your proposed topic– to everyone interested. You'll find that a media kit will be a helpful advertisement of yourself to send to prospective talk shows. While large companies will invest a lot of money in a sophisticated and attractive media kit to promote their company, product or service, yours needn't be expensive in order to be effective. But it should include the following materials:

- **Press release:** An informative article or announcement designed to notify the media about your latest work– or whatever project is motivating you to seek a talk show appearance. Always include a press release in your media kit, even if you haven't sent it to any media.

- **Biography:** Relevant information about your life and career.

- **Endorsements:** Letters of recommendation from recognizable names or celebrities, or from authorities who support your work or you personally.

- **Testimonials:** Letters of recommendation from past clients and people who have used your product or services, or support your cause, and have positive comments.

- **Reprints:** Articles you've written, or articles that have been written about or focus on you and your work. Copies, rather than originals, are fine.

- **List of other media appearances:** Include program names, station call letters and cities, or names of networks and dates of interview.

- **Calendar:** Your upcoming travel schedule for the next few months.

- **Your book, video tape, audio cassette:** Include a sample of your product, if available. True, most producers and hosts will only skim through a few pages of your book, watch your video for a moment, or briefly listen to a few minutes of your tape. But there's no better proof of your credibility than this tangible product. If you're going to send an audio tape, please place it in its own insulated jiffy bag to assure safe arrival. I have a drawer filled with broken plastic and mangled tape to prove that this advice warrants giving.

- **Photo:** A black-and-white photo of yourself, if available.

In addition, you should put some careful thought in developing the following materials for your media kit. Your objective here is to provide as much support, justification and information as possible to assure the producer that yours would indeed be a successful and entertaining appearance. Don't give the producer a reason to say no to you!

1. Write a cover letter...and mention immediately that you are sending the information at the request of the producer. Stations receive sacks of mail every day– most of it is thrown out after a five-second glance to see whether it was solicited. You'll earn extra points if you point out how your appearance would be of value to the show. (WII-FM works both ways!) *excuse content*

2. Develop a list of different angles, slants or hooks for your interview. This will further ensure the likelihood that you'll fulfill a need. While an interview with an office decorator might not fuel the producer's interest, a discussion about how colors and lighting can stimulate productivity in the workplace might be a topic he knows his audience will be interested in. If you're an expert in more than one area, bring this to the attention of the producer. If you've been on a panel or another talk show to speak about a different topic, be sure to include this as well.

3. Generate a list of recommended questions that the talk show host might ask you during an interview. (You may include answers as well.) As you develop your questions, make sure you're prepared to answer them in a lively, conversational manner, and that at least some questions lead into good anecdotal material. Don't write close-ended questions that can only be answered with a "Yes" or "No." Make sure your questions are succinct, short and to the point. Do not write "run-on," paragraph-length questions. Remember, the host may very well ask you these questions on the air, and he must weave your questions into his conversation in a smooth, natural way.

A final word on your media kit: Don't overwhelm the producer with paper. Exclusive of a book or tape, all your material should fit easily within a standard-size folder. If you have reams of testimonials, for example, just send the one or two best. A producer who's responsible for generating 100 to 300 talk shows a year simply doesn't have the time to read through piles of material.

Follow-up is a must

Always follow up with a telephone call about a week after you expect your media kit landed on your contact's desk. Don't wait for the producer to call you back. Trust me: Someone else will be more aggressive than you and push hard for the producer's attention. You have to participate in the game the same way if you expect to be heard. Your behavior will not be considered too aggressive by the producer (unless you are obnoxious *and* pushy).

If the producer informs you that a decision has not yet been made or that he or she hasn't yet examined your media kit, fine! Simply thank him or her and schedule a follow-up call in another week. Then follow through. Continue this until you have an acceptance...or a rejection. Always be courteous, but don't ever settle for a "we'll call you if we're interested" attitude.

I am always unimpressed and somewhat amused by the many people who make an original contact to get on *"Your Own Success,"* and then never follow up. As I discard their voluminous media kits, I often wonder if they are still in business or interested in the publicity I could have offered. There simply isn't enough time for me to call everyone who has submitted material, especially if I am currently booked solid. There is no doubt in my mind that some of the discarded material could have evolved into good interviews.

But I have learned from past experience that newer material, just as good, will find its way to my desk. Thus, the older material gets tossed.

As you are in discussion with producers, you may hear many viable reasons about why your interview just isn't right for that show. Some producers may truly believe that you would make a good guest, but can't go forward because they feel it necessary to expand the topic with other compatible guests. It's likely in these cases that time limitations are the real problem, and there just isn't enough of it to find these missing links.

If you find yourself in such a situation, why not suggest that the project be placed on your shoulders? After all, who knows more about finding compatible guests than you? Whatever your topic, you certainly know it inside and out! If the opposing view is wanted by the producer, volunteer to find the qualified candidates and to do all the ground work to bring your talk show interview to life.

I have asked potential guests to develop the suggested segment for me only three times, but all three times I was pleasantly surprised at the outcome. If you're being rejected just because the producer is just too busy to do all the work, offer to help. You may be granted an interview as the direct result of your efforts.

A final caveat: Don't pay for your interview!

Fortunately, it's rare for a station to request that you pay *them* for your interview. If it does occur– and it may– it will probably be in radio or some local cable TV systems, hardly ever in broadcast television. Only stations with ratings slightly below sea level– which means virtually no one is listening to their programs– would suggest that you pay. Because these stations have no audience, they can't sell advertising. The editorial portions of their programming– the talk show you thought you wanted to appear on– is all they *can* sell.

Don't get stuck paying for an interview. The cycle in which these stations participate is a vicious one. They have few listeners because the programming is so bad. The programming is bad because they'll take anybody's money and allow them to talk about anything. There is no program flow or continuity. As a result, they can't attract a base of listeners because they don't appeal to a specific audience with specific interests. Your paid interview on this type of station will most likely be sandwiched between topics having no flow into, or out of, *your* topic.

On the other hand, don't ever expect to get *paid* for an interview, either! When you hint at or outright request payment for an interview, you are immediately branded a rank amateur. As we've already discussed, radio and television talk shows are a great way to get your message across to an interested and large audience. You will have to work hard at getting yourself on talk shows and putting out an effective message, but it should all be worth your while when the phones ring and the mail pours in from interested buyers of your services and products. *That* is how you get paid for your efforts.

When you reach the top of the talk show ladder and you are invited to participate on national television network shows, you may actually be given a nominal scale payment. But even then, your motivation should be to get the word out to potential clients and buyers, not to collect a fee.

How long does all this take?

The time lag between your first conversation with a producer and the actual time of the interview is usually about four to six weeks. But, you shouldn't be discouraged if it takes longer to get an affirmative response to your request for an interview. Continue to stay in contact with the producer, provide updated materials as appropriate. And be persistent...without being a pest.

It *will* all pay off for you.

Chapter 4

Preparing For Your Appearance

Congratulations! You got the interview! Your research, pavement-pounding and door-knocking have paid off. You deserve to celebrate. But once you finish the champagne and shake off the confetti, be prepared to roll up your sleeves and start readying yourself for your appearance. Your work has just begun.

Confirm your arrangement with the station

When you are invited to interview, either by phone or letter, you should send the station a letter of confirmation, listing all the details as you understand them. You might receive such a letter from the producer, but this practice is usually followed only in major market and national programs. As you prepare your letter, a number of questions may arise. Be sure you get answers as soon as possible.

1. *Will the program be a live, real-time show, or will it be taped for future play back?*

If the program is live, which most are apt to be, you have a great opportunity to be very topical in your discussion. You can mention dates for seminars you're conducting, speeches you're giving, or special events you're sponsoring.

2. *Will I be interviewed alone, or will I be part of a panel discussion?*

It's infinitely better to be the sole guest rather than a member of a panel. On radio, many people sound alike, and trying to match people's voices to words can sometimes be difficult for home listeners. The publicity value and your time on the air shrink, and the clarity of the interview diminishes as well.

3. *Will I be in the studio or will this be a telephone interview? (radio only)*

Besides the comfort of interviewing from home, you can accomplish just as much in a "phoner" interview as in a live one. State-of-the-art radio technology is such that most listeners can't differentiate one from the other. Listen carefully the next time *you're* tuned to a radio talk show— you'll probably find it next to impossible to distinguish a phone interview from a live one.

4. *Will the host open up the conversation to telephone calls?*

If you are expected to talk with listeners, you have the chance to make your points directly to the individuals who call, and to come across as more personable.

5. *How much time are you slotting for my interview?*

You will want to know how long you're expected to be on the air so you can plan your presentation appropriately. However, a producer can only "guesstimate" each segment's air time. The average broadcast day is subject to more unexpected changes than any other business. Hot news stories, local weather changes, long-winded talent, and a host of other unexpected situations can, and probably will, arise. The best you can do is put up with this reality and shine when it's your time.

One cautionary note: If the show is going long and it appears your expected 20 minutes is about to become two, it's not unreasonable to ask if you can come back again.

6. *May I give out my toll-free number or local number?*

On radio, most producers will allow you to give out your telephone number. If you're doing a telephone interview on a station in another state, don't expect your local telephone number to ring off the hook. It is best in this case to use an 800 number service, or have the station refer calls to you. On television, to avoid clutter, some producers will not allow you to give out your telephone number. In these instances, ask for mail to be forwarded to you by the station.

It is crucial that you secure some sort of system for listeners and viewers to reach you, post-interview. Don't settle for nebulous responses like, "Remind me about that, the day of the interview," or, "That's not our policy, but I'll see what I can do." Remember, the producer is not necessarily focused on *your* interests. It is up to *you* to be insistent about setting up a response vehicle, whether it's mentioning your phone number or directing the audience to write to you in care of the station.

7. *Are there any chances for a sports preemption? (radio only)*

Chances of preemption? If you're scheduled on an AM station that carries local sporting events, you should know that there is as much as a 50 percent *likelihood* of preemption if the program falls during a time when a game might be played. Most program directors schedule these revenue-generating events at the beginning of the season and update weekly to accommodate rain-outs and changes. If your appearance is scheduled during the time a game might be broadcast, ask the producer or call the station's sports department about the likelihood of preemption.

Four Questions You Should *Never* Ask

Equally important as knowing the right questions to ask about your upcoming interview is knowing which questions *not* to ask. High on the producer frustration meter are these questions, too frequently asked by naive guests:

1. *How much air time will I be guaranteed?*

Radio and TV stations are under great time restraints. You may be booked for a 20-minute segment, but because of problems beyond anyone's control, actually get only four or five minutes of air time. Asking for an exact amount of time for your interview is asking the producer to promise you something he simply can't control. On the other hand, your appearance may be so wonderful that the host will not want to let you go. To a certain extent, you influence, by your effectiveness, how long you'll be on the air once you get there.

2. *What should I say?*

If you convey to the producer and host that you don't know what to say, chances are they will reconsider interviewing you. They want someone who has a strong opinion, who is driven to share this opinion with the audience and who is assured and interesting. Asking "What should I say?," is like asking a waitress "What do I want for breakfast?"

3. *How should I act?*

Once again, this question will raise doubts about your potential as an effective guest. When in doubt, always act as yourself or as you would if you were home having a conversation with friends. One of the biggest mistakes guests make is to assume they must "act" at all.

4. *What is the station wattage? (radio)*

This question came into vogue a few years ago and has driven radio producers and hosts crazy ever since. Asking this question to show that you know something about radio just shows that the *opposite* is true. Wattage is only one of many characteristics of a radio station's signal that apply to its coverage or reach. The uninformed inquirer usually assumes that low wattage means that the station is small (because its signal is weak). This is not true, however, because a low-watt station on an exceptionally high tower will cover more distance than a high-watt station on a very low tower. And without knowing the other characteristics of the signal, this information is useless– it's like asking what size tires a car has in order to determine the car's speed.

Get to know your audience

Now that you know a little more about the circumstances of your interview– from approximately how long you're expected to talk to whether you'll be sharing the stage with other panelists– you're ready to prepare further for your upcoming appearance. You should spend some time, at this point, in learning what you can about the audience you'll be reaching.

You probably already know something about your audience, through the research you did while trying to obtain an invitation from the station. It's helpful to know, for example, the average age or age range of the audience, as well as educational background, occupation and even buying habits. If the typical listener of the radio talk show you're appearing on is 35 years old, female, employed in a professional or business capacity and spends more than the average on clothing, you may tailor the information you relay about your personal shopping service a little differently than you would if you were talking to 65-year-old men who spend their disposable income on home-improvement projects. You can find out most of this valuable information from the station's media kit, which is normally used to attract advertisers.

But there's something even more basic that you should know about radio and TV audiences– a fascinating secret that will enhance your media interviews' effectiveness tenfold. For reasons I do not fully comprehend, this fact never seems to find its way to talk show guests. Yet, as you can see, the information is first and foremost on the minds of every broadcast producer and host. If you observe them doing their jobs, you'll notice that they give away their secret readily.

The next time you listen to the radio or watch television, count the number of times the broadcast station identifies itself. Talk radio stations identify their call letters on the average of once every five minutes, more if the host can manage to squeeze it in. Music stations usually manage to name the call letters before and after each song played, about every two to three minutes. Television stations identify themselves usually at the beginning and end of each pod of commercials. Some of the newer 24-hour cable television networks such as MTV and VH-1 actually have a transparent network logo visible at *all* times except during commercials.

Why this repetitive identification? Simple. Broadcasters know that most listeners and viewers don't tune in at the beginning of a program and stay with it until it's over. TV audiences, for example, tend to tune in on the half-hour. While a significant percentage may watch a half-hour program from beginning to end, most are likely to flip between channels, at least during commercials.

Radio audiences are even more fickle. They don't tune in at any particular time. They find new programs when they are tired or bored with the one they're listening to. Consider that a large piece of the radio audience pie tunes in when driving. Listeners may get into their car 15 minutes before the hour to get to work. They may flip through stations trying to find a traffic or weather report, switching to their favorite talk show or music program after they get the information they needed. It's not difficult to believe the industry data that indicates a highly transient audience.

It's important for broadcasters to reach as many people as possible, whenever they tune in, with their most important message— who they are. Because the call letters are what is reported to the ratings services.

So, take your cue from the broadcast stations. *Repeat yourself, and do it often.* Identify your most important points and reiterate them frequently during your interview.

If your TV interview is scheduled to begin late into the first half-hour— 8:20 or 8:25, for example— and extend into the next half hour, you should repeat the significant points you made in the first segment after the commercial break. You can be sure that many new viewers tuned in to your interview at the half- hour mark. If you are interviewed on a radio talk show for 20 minutes, you should *know* that many new listeners are tuning in throughout your conversation. Repeat your most important points, three or four times if you can.

Promote your appearance in advance

Remember, you want to reach as many people as possible who are interested in the service or products you supply or the cause you're promoting. Therefore, it stands to reason that you should do everything in your power to attract those listeners or viewers to your interview. A listing in a local newspaper may attract the attention of dozens of individuals who will tune in just to hear your segment.

Contact the public relations department of the radio or TV station to see how they may help your cause. You should ask that your particular interview be mentioned in any upcoming press releases or newspaper listings. But don't rely on the TV or radio station to do all your promotion for you. Work to get the right people to listen or view your interview. If you are so inclined and knowledgeable, you may send out a brief press release to local newspapers announcing the fact that you will be a guest on the upcoming program.

If you are addressing any group before the interview, be sure to mention the program. If you are a member of an organization that has monthly meetings, be sure to announce your interview and, perhaps, publicize it in your organization's monthly newsletter. If you can obtain a mailing list of members, create and mail a flier.

Prime the pump

"Priming the pump" is an effective principle that television producers appreciate well. Most of the original television programs were just televised radio shows with live audiences. If someone said something funny, the audience would naturally laugh. When things became somewhat more sophisticated, producers filmed situation comedies without audiences, and soon found the need for canned laughter and, later, the well-known audio laugh track. The laugh track was originally designed to clue the audience to laugh, or prime the pump. The technique is still used today, and we take this absurdity for granted.

But take advantage of the prime-the-pump principle. If your host is going to open the interview to telephone callers, get a friend or two to call you on the program. Assign them actual questions to ask you on the air. Many times listeners won't call a new voice unless they hear someone else do it first. Usually, one set-up call will do the trick, but it's wise to have a few waiting just in case. Additionally, these set-up calls assure you of two things: That you will receive phone calls (imagine the painful silence if the phone never rings during your interview), and that you'll be able to answer at least some questions with ease and confidence, bolstering your credibility to other listeners.

One important caution: Most on-air radio telephone numbers are not the same as the main switchboard numbers. So be sure you give the *correct* number to your set-up callers.

Feeling lucky?

Here's how you can turn an interview that's good for the station into an interview that's good for you, too: Whatever it is you actually do, prepare a very brief report with an intriguing topic and title. Make sure that your report relates in some way to your on-the-air discussion. For example, if you are a sales trainer sharing the secrets of sales success, put together a report entitled "How to guarantee 100% more commission dollars in ten easy steps." Include the secrets that work for you. Relay the shortcuts that have taken you years to learn. Put *real value* into the report and give it away– yes, free of charge– to any listener who calls you.

Let me demonstrate the power of these free reports, which I call "luck makers" (you'll soon see why). I was a consultant a few years ago for a low-priced stock newsletter. The company used TV and radio advertising to sell subscriptions. I realized immediately that the ads needed to generate a lot more excitement than they did. I suggested including a free report called "The 10 stocks that are poised to double in value this year." After assuring that reliable information could be obtained, the editorial staff researched and identified stocks that were targeted to double in value in a very short time. The final report was finished in a few days and the free offer was edited into the existing commercials.

In just three weeks, the response rate more than *quadrupled* and two-year subscriptions were up over 100 percent! Thousands of dollars in profits began coming in daily. We didn't change the ad copy, or lower the price, or change the product. We simply included a free report that cost us a few pennies each to produce. As a result, handsome profits were produced overnight.

You can enjoy the same response by being clever and giving honest information to all viewers and listeners. Remember, each request will cost you the price of a first-class stamp, so you might want to consider asking for a stamped, self-addressed envelope. Although this will significantly reduce your response, it will also help to weed out the professional "freebie" hunters who will send for anything. I don't recommend one method over the other– it comes down to how much you can afford to invest in marketing yourself.

I currently give these free reports away to any *"Your Own Success"* listener who sends us a stamped self-addressed envelope: "How to Start a Business in Your Spare Time," "The 12 Keys to Personal and Professional Success," "How and Where to Find Venture Capital," and, the Goethe quote, "Begin it Now," in calligraphy form. I am not looking to sell the respondents a product; rather, I am selling our show, and ensuring their continued listenership. This little exercise keeps the listeners involved in the program and gives them added value. I have received thousands of requests and, therefore, have retained thousands of involved listeners.

Create your *own* luck maker

I once interviewed an insurance sales representative on the topic of retirement planning. This is not an especially scintillating topic and I was worried that things would get a little boring. But, happily, the guest surprised me. He revealed that the Social Security Agency is making serious mistakes in more than 10 percent of all accounts. "In other words," he continued, "over 10 percent of everyone listening to my voice probably has some problem in the account containing your retirement money."

The phones started ringing immediately! "What can I do about it?," the listeners wanted to know. He was ready for them. He explained that if everyone concerned about retirement planning were to call his 800 telephone number, he would supply them, free of charge, with a special postage-paid postcard that would obligate the Social Security Administration to send them an analysis of their holdings.

By day's end, more than 600 people called him. And the calls continued long after the segment aired. By the time the siege was over, he had more than 1,800 respondents to his offer. This was with only *one* toll-free line and, remember, this response came from New York City only.

P.S.: What he *didn't* tell the audience that day was that anybody can call the local Social Security office and request this free service.

Nevertheless, his clever thinking and helpful service provided him with the names, addresses and phone numbers of more than 1,800 potential clients. Needless to say, he was able to sell lots of insurance as a result of his luckmaker.

More clever marketing

Elysa Lazar, publisher of the quarterly newsletter, *Mail Order Shopping!,* was invited to appear on a *"Good Morning America"* feature about trends in home shopping. Her involvement amounted to little more than 20 seconds of the final edited piece, but, to her surprise, she was able to convince the powers-that-be to make the following offer, which was announced at the close of the piece: "If you would like a sample copy of Mail Order Shopper, send $1.50 to the following address..."

Less than a week later, she received a call from a local postal supervisor asking for a meeting. She asked why. "So that we can agree about what you would like us to do with your mail," came the polite response. "Just bring it up, like you always do," said Elysa. So all 70,000 pieces were promptly delivered by a regiment of burly and somewhat confused mailmen.

That's not the end of the story. As I write this, six months after the interview played, Ms. Lazar reports that more than four percent has converted to annual subscribers (a very high direct-response conversion rate) and she continues to receive between 25 and 100 responses each week, most still containing $1.50 in cash, coin and stamps.

If you're an author, or you're promoting a training video, you can achieve extra interview clout by devising a clever way to give away your product. Suggest to the host your willingness to give a copy or two of your books or tapes to a few lucky listeners.

One possibility: Suggest that you ask listeners or viewers a question that might be answered by referring to your book, video or tape. The conversation from that point will center on your work, and there will be plenty of opportunities to give out the name of your work, and your telephone number.

What will I say? How will I act?

Do these questions sound familiar? They should. They're two of the four questions I advised you *never* to ask a producer. Yet, in order to have a successful interview, you'd better ask them of yourself– and have some pretty good answers! What you say, and, even more important, how you present that information, is key to your interview success.

Of course, you will not be following a script, and the course of the interview will be influenced largely by the producer, the host, the call-ins and other factors outside your control. Yet you should prepare yourself by identifying what information you intend to impart– and how you can most effectively communicate it. Following are several tips for you to consider while you're preparing for your appearance:

Be yourself. Don't try to "act" like you're doing a talk show interview. Try to think of the interview as a coffee-table conversation with friends. You will come across as genuine and credible if you prepare yourself to "act" naturally.

Pace yourself. Most radio stations program five or six commercial breaks per hour. Weather checks, traffic updates, sports updates, time checks and station identifications that break up the remaining editorial minutes. Television stations and cable networks, as well, break up their programming with commercials, station identification and public service announcements.

What does all this mean to you? It means get to the point...quickly. Prepare your material in short, two- or three-minute modules. There is no time to develop stories or to give long-winded presentations. Nothing is more frustrating to listeners than to hear a story develop, only to be interrupted by a commercial break. When this happens, the story never seems to get back on track and everyone gets annoyed. This is the reason that public speakers and full-day seminar leaders who are trained to pace audiences over much longer periods of time have so much trouble in media interviews.

Speak in least common denominator-ese. Consider the fraction 48/64. Try to visualize, if you will, 48/64 of a pie. It doesn't bring to mind a clear picture, does it? How about 24/32? It's still too much pie to picture clearly. 12/16? A little better, but not as clear as 6/8. And 6/8 is not as instantly visual as 3/4. Now, 3/4 of a pie is something we can sink our teeth into!

Reducing the fraction to its lowest common denominator results in a clear picture of how much pie we have— three pieces out of four, three-quarters, 75 percent. While 48/64, 24/32, 12/16, 6/8, and 3/4 all mean the same thing, 3/4— the least common denominator— is the easiest to picture.

The same is true of words. While you want to appear intelligent and authoritative, you don't have to do it by using big words (I *could* have said polysyllabic words) and long, compound sentences. In reality, you'll communicate more effectively if you communicate more simply.

I once heard a talk show guest, a career counsellor, say something like, "The worth of an honorable and conscientious individual is measured by his or her abilities to carry out obligations as requested by his or her corporate superiors." What he meant was "You'll get ahead if you do what your boss wants." Which communicates more clearly— 27 words with eight multi-syllable words, or nine words with one two-syllable word?

Here's a helpful self-check: Take your list of questions that you will supply to the producer and write out your answers the way you perceive yourself responding. Get rid of all the four-syllable words and most of the three-syllable words. Pretend that you are addressing your response to a group of ten-year olds. Don't be concerned about talking down to your audience. Just pick up a copy of the *Wall Street Journal,* a sophisticated and highly respected daily read by educated and successful business people. You'll discover that the editors of this publication have learned the importance of writing in least common denominator-ese. Anyone with a high school education can read and appreciate it.

Avoid "yes" and "no" answers. While you are preparing to speak understandably, using simple words and short, clear sentences, you should remind yourself to steer away from "yes" or "no" answers or one- or two-word responses. Even if your host asks close-ended questions such as "Do you like what you do?" you should prepare to elaborate. Rather than responding with a quick, "yes," you might reply, "I like my job so much that..." or "What makes my job so enjoyable is..." Limiting your responses to one-word answers is the easiest way to guarantee a short or aborted interview.

And the greatest talk show secret...

Sell without selling. How many times have you witnessed the obnoxious guest who obviously has only one agenda, to sell and sell hard? He holds up books and tapes, one after another, espousing platitude after trite platitude interwoven into limitless 800 telephone numbers. It's worse than a bad commercial!

"Yippie"-turned-entrepreneur Jerry Rubin was my worst interview nightmare. He just couldn't stop selling! His few moments of editorial comments, which reflected his brilliance, were overshadowed by nearly 40 minutes of hard-sell. We actually had to tell him, on the air, to stop selling!

The greatest talk-show secret is, without a doubt, to sell by *not* selling. "But Al," you ask, "haven't you been telling me throughout this book that the true value of a talk show interview is in increasing exposure to my product? In generating more business? In *selling?*"

Yes, indeed! And I don't take back one word of it! You want your interview to generate interest– and requests– for your service or product. But what you don't want is to turn off your potential customers with an offensive hard-sell. Give your audience information, raise questions, create a need. Then provide answers– as our insurance salesman did so effectively when he informed his listeners about the Social Security situation, then told them how they could find out about their accounts.

Learn to weave your sales points into your discussion. Example: A speech coach and author might say, "In my book, *Speaking Without Fear*, I mention the eight ways to control breathing." This brings the message home powerfully, without sounding like a hard-sell. Serve your listeners -- and you'll serve yourself.

What the experts say

It's interesting to see how some very savvy, experienced interviewers prepare themselves for guesting opportunities.

As you read their comments, ask yourself if a particular style feels comfortable for you, then adopt it with the confidence that it works for someone who has tested the waters for you.

Visualization is a concept that is often used by veteran talk show guests to prepare for upcoming interviews. Co-author of the best-selling *One Minute Manager,* Ken Blanchard takes this a step further saying, "I visualize the end of the show with the host saying what a great interview it has been. Then I see as I walk out, people patting me on the back and saying, 'That was great!' If I visualize the end first, then I begin to move towards that picture."

One of the great gentleman guests, author of mega-selling *The Greatest Salesman in The World*, Og Mandino says, "I review several pages of notes before each program so that I'll be able to handle just about any question."

Another veteran television performer, puppeteer-comedian Shari Lewis offers this sage advice, "Before the show, I do not concentrate on what I have to say. I focus on the fact that I'm going to have a lovely interaction with the host. I commit myself to sincerity in conveying my information, and in my relationship with the host."

Motivational author Skip Cypert says, "I have a guidepost, a short succinct central theme around which I can build my message."

Barbara Brabec is an expert on starting and operating home businesses, an in-demand topic for radio talk shows. She says, "I prepare by finding out what they want me to address, then I keep a little reminder sheet by the phone to save as a memory refresher for me."

Robert Half, creator of Robert Half International, the worldwide recruitment firm, and an astute guest, offers, "If the subject of the interview is not fresh in my mind, I'll read my notes several times, and even listen to an audio or video of me being interviewed on that particular subject. I always believe I won't remember a thing. But I always do. I would urge the reader not to try to memorize. Too often, when you attempt to memorize, you're memorizing words instead of thoughts, and you just won't come across as well." Mr. Half is on target: I have witnessed many guests, especially those new to the game, make this mistake.

One of my favorite response comes from Dr. Lane Longfellow, a professional personal development speaker, author and seminar leader. "I don't prepare," says Longfellow, "I prefer to let the energy of the moment come through. That's risky. Sometimes I lose." I like his response because it's completely consistent with his "on stage" performance philosophy.

Best-selling management author and in-demand speaker Tom Peters shows his understanding of the media by his response, "I go over in my mind a half-dozen or so key points, trying to invent memorable 'sound bites' ahead of time." A sound bite is a few words that vividly and easily define a more confusing theme. Perhaps his most famous is "management by wandering around" or as he calls it MBWA.

We're all familiar with President Bush's contributions to memorable sound bites, such as his "thousand points of light" and "read my lips." The media is obsessed in finding and exploiting sound bites. If you can create them as well as Tom Peters and President Bush, you will be ahead of the game. Dottie Walters, co-author of *Speak and Grow Rich,* also uses sound bites, such as "there could be money in your mouth."

One of the truly natural talk show guests is Stew Leonard. Stew owns a dairy store in Norwalk, Conn., which in itself would not seem to be the stuff of talk shows. Until, that is, you visit the store. The best way to describe the experience is like taking a trip to Disneyland. Stew's happiness and enthusiasm about his business is infectious. There's nothing phony about him. He's learned how to make grocery shopping fun and he reaps the benefits in that his store grosses almost $100 million annually. In preparing for an interview, Stew says, "I try to get myself up by re-reading all the best material that has ever been written about our store. I also have an 'inspiration book,' a three-ring binder that has my collection of quotes I've saved for the occasion over the years."

Carole Hyatt, co-author of **When Smart People Fail** and author of **Changing Gears,** cautions those published talk show guests. "Particularly in the beginning of a book tour, I find that I had worked on the book almost a year before, and sometimes two years, and have literally forgotten what's in the book. So, I reread the book, and take index-card notes on the book and bring my own copy of the book so that I can follow the host." I am constantly surprised at how many times I've seen the "Fear of God" on the faces of authors I'm interviewing, as I say something like, "Let's talk about the five ways to keep your memory from failing you as you discussed in your book."

Austin McGonigle, one of the world's leading sales trainers has an interesting philosophy for preparing for interviews. He says, "I get calm and remember all the people I have positively influenced with my advice and direction." Austin has hit the proverbial nail on the head with his simple but powerful advice.

Richard Lederer, a talk show host's dream, is the author of **Anguished English, Crazy English, Play of Words** and **Take Thee to a Punnery.** In his 28-plus years as a teacher, he has collected thousands of examples of the most humorous mangled phrases, mixed metaphors and dangling participles known to man. How does he prepare for an interview? "I memorize a great deal of the material from the book to be talked about, find out all I can about the interviewers, their program and the specific audiences. I adapt material as much as I can for that show."

His work pays off: He's always ready with rapid-fire responses. Ask him, for example, of a memorable metaphor, and he snaps back with a quote from Lou Brock, famous St.

Louis Cardinals outfielder: "I always felt I was a guy who had the ability to light the spark of enthusiasm which unlocked the hidden geysers of adrenalin that causes one to play to the summit of his ability."

Warren Bennis, the distinguished professor of business administration at the University of Southern California, responds with an answer briefer than his title. "I think about the simplest way I can present the basic ideas." (Remember least-common-denominator-ese?)

A before-the-interview checklist

1. Are you familiar with the talk show on which you're going to appear? Do you know the host's name, the format and what is expected of you?
2. Do you know who your audience is?
3. Have you taken advantage of every opportunity to promote your appearance?
4. Have you rehearsed answering all possible questions that may be asked of you?
5. Do you know the major point(s) you wish to make? And are you prepared to repeat them several times? Have you practiced pacing yourself? Are you prepared to speak in least-common-denominator-ese?
6. If your interview includes call-ins, have you contacted two or three friends to call in with prepared questions (prime that pump!)?
7. Do you have your 800 or local telephone number and mailing address ready?
8. Have you prepared your luck-maker?
9. Do you have a copy of your book (speech, audiotape, videotape, product, etc.)?
10. Can you explain what you do in one brief sentence?
11. Have you asked "What's in it for me?" (WII-FM) Do you have an answer?

The pre-interview: Your dress rehearsal

Many top television talk shows and a growing number of radio talk shows have instituted a practice of conducting pre-interviews. This is usually done by telephone, but, on occasion, you will be invited into the studio to meet personally with a producer. He or she will ask many questions about your topic to see how much depth you have so that the host can be prepared. Here is your chance to "show your stuff!"

Consider the pre-interview a dress rehearsal. The producer is making mental notes about how your answers will flow with the personality of the host. If you are familiar with the host, you should answer as if you were talking with him or her directly. "It's okay to fumble, but it's *not* okay to stop talking" is the cardinal rule of pre-interviews.

Don't confuse pre-interviews with auditions. When you are invited to a pre-interview, you have essentially been chosen as a qualified guest for the show. Go in with confidence that the producer wants you. Don't fear being rejected at this point.

But don't get cocky, either. Changes *can* still be made to the guest list!

Chapter 5

Countdown To Air Time

Today's the day! You've prepared your answers to anticipated questions. You have your materials together. You've practiced a confident and polished, but friendly and natural, demeanor as you've rehearsed potential interview scenarios with your spouse or in front of the mirror. You've anticipated the deluge of phone calls or mail in response to your interview. (Admit it: You've even imagined yourself being asked to host the *"Tonight Show,"* or maybe receiving a movie offer.)

But in the few hours you have before you appear on the air, you can still do a lot to maximize your experience and get the most out of your interview.

Stage fright? Join the club!

Your hands sweat. Your heart races. Your stomach flip-flops. And as you anticipate your impending appearance— the interview you've worked so hard to obtain— you decide sitting through a series of root canals may be a preferable alternative to your possible humiliation in front of an audience of tens or hundreds of thousands of strangers.

You are not alone if you feel nervous about guesting on radio or television talk shows. I asked experienced guests about their greatest fears before appearing on radio or television talk shows. Here are just a few of their responses:

- Famed attorney Roy Grutman responded that his greatest fear was "that I might be in an ambush."

- Jonathan Evetts, author of ***The Seven Pillars of Sales Success,*** fears "being forced to tailor 25 years of sales research and experience to the hosts' immature misconceptions of selling."

- Ted Dreier, author of ***Take Your Life Off Hold,*** worries "that my mind would go blank, that I would use poor grammar, that I would say something stupid."

- Stan Katz, co-author of ***The Success Trap,*** fears "hosts who are more interested in themselves than their guests."

- Ken Blanchard, claims his greatest fear is "that the interviewer will get you off on some tangent which will make it hard to get back to the main reason for your appearance."

- Jeanette Reddish Scollard, entrepreneur and author of ***Risk To Win***, reveals a unique concern. Her attractiveness seems to generate questions about her personal life. "I've learned how to avoid answering them," she quickly adds.

- Og Mandino, author of ***The Greatest Salesman in the World***, reflects a concern common to guests who interview frequently when he responds, "that I'll repeat myself. Often when doing eight or nine shows in a day, one hears a question and hesitates before answering ... because he thinks he just said that... and yet he didn't say it here... he said it on a previous show, an hour ago, down the street."

- Shari Lewis reports her fear "that a dull/inexperienced/disinterested host will do a tedious interview and, as a result, I will sound boring."

- Harry Lorayne, the world's foremost memory expert, told me that he still checks to see if his fly is open before a TV guest appearance.

As you read through these, I hope you gained some comfort from knowing that any fears you have about interviewing are shared by some of the biggest names in the business. I read somewhere that even Johnny Carson has fear anxieties. A while back, he volunteered to be wired for an experiment. What the experiement revealed was surprising. Apparently, as he first steps out of the curtain and faces the audience, his heartbeat races to almost double the norm. And that's after more than 30 years of on-camera experience!

Yes, even those of us on the other side of the guest chair experience stage fright. For more than a year after I began co-hosting *"Your Own Success,"* I would wake up in the middle of the night with the show on my mind and the awareness that I'd be on the air in a few hours. The only time I could relax was at the beginning of the program when I knew everything was under control. Herein lies the great wisdom. Despite any pre-show jitters you may experience, the better prepared you are, the more likely you'll relax once you're on the air.

I interviewed one gentleman who started out as a door-to-door encyclopedia salesman and eventually came to own the company. I mentioned this to the audience, turned to him and asked him to share his feelings of accomplishment. His mouth opened as if to respond...and he said nothing. I realized after a few seconds that he was literally paralyzed with fear, so I answered my own question. He recovered instantly, and proceeded to provide a fascinating and entertaining interview.

Bert Decker, personal communications expert, told me that he and his wife, Deborah, were reviewing a tape of a TV interview they had recently completed. He noticed that his wife had casually placed her hand on her chest, where she kept it during most of the interview. As they reviewed the interview, she confided to him that she had been so overcome with nervousness that she felt compelled to cover her heart. She was sure that it must be visibly pounding from her chest!

I share these two incidents to illustrate a lesson to be learned: Your fears are generally much more apparent to you than to anyone else. Just remember: The home viewers or listeners are not aware of your nervousness. There's no need to call attention to the fact. Don't apologize for a shaky voice, and don't draw attention to your sweating palms.

What you can do to reduce stress

When I asked famous stress expert Dr. Peter Hanson how he prepares for his many radio and television interviews, he referred me to his best-selling book, *Stress for Success*. "Plan ahead by eating a light snack that is high in fiber, such as whole-wheat bread and an apple, several hours before you are due to go on. Do not eat anything fatty, or heavy with protein, or too great in quantity. If you do, your stomach may be competing with the audience for your attention. Avoid all caffeine, as it will exaggerate all the stress responses by causing enormous surges of adrenaline and other hormones. Endorphine, the body's own molecule of morphine, has great powers to calm jangled nerves. Slow abdominal breathing, exercise earlier in the day, or even massaging one of the acupuncture pressure points (such as the "V" between the base of the thumb and index fingers, or the shoulder tips) can all prove effective and yet socially acceptable ways to get the endorphine going. Except for vigorous exercise, all these techniques can be used right up until the last moments before you are introduced to the audience."

Actor, raconteur, author and pioneer talk show guest Orson Bean has some helpful, down-to-earth advice on pre-interview stage fright: "You will be nervous or frightened before being interviewed, in all probability. Instead of saying to yourself, 'Why can't I be cool, laid-back and relaxed?' Face the fact that it is exciting to be on the radio or TV. We want to feel in control so we clamp down" Orson, who diagnoses stage fright as "excitement clamped-down" advises talk show guests to take deep breaths to avoid this syndrome.

So as you make your final preparations for your appearance, don't let nervousness spoil the experience for you. Take a deep breath and remind yourself that you've prepared for this exciting moment.

And enjoy it!

Dress to impress

Of course, you already know how important your appearance is to the impact of your interview, particularly if you are guesting on a television talk show. And I'll assume that you know what appropriate attire is, whether you're CEO of a Fortune 500 company or president of an entrepreneurial enterprise that trains clowns. But you should be aware that TV appearances pose some unique challenges to dressing effectively— and comfortably.

Lights are probably the biggest challenge. Shari Lewis gives this advice: "Remember that the lights are hot and you will perspire! Don't bring wool suits or sweaters to your interview— wear thin, light, bright fabrics that breathe. You will be better able to concentrate on your task at hand if you're not conscious of sweat dribbling down the bridge of your nose."

In my 10 years of producing television talk shows and as an observer of other producers' work, I continue to see the same wardrobe mistakes over and over again. So here's my brief advice on the topic.

- Before any TV program, every male guest should go out and purchase the longest pair of socks he can find. Nothing is more distracting to the viewer than a hairy band of skin between the top of the socks and pant cuffs.

- Avoid anything that can be described as "herringbone." This pattern comes to life, causing a strange, animated optical effect that becomes an irritating challenge for the cameraman.

- Do not choose to wear a black or stark-white outfit, because they tend to blend in with the furniture and background. You want the audience to be able to see where *you* end and the couch *begins*. Blues and grays always work. Men should choose an off-color shirt, not a white one.

- Avoid shiny fabrics because the camera has a problem defining reflections. Sometimes they appear to be smudges or stains on your clothes.

- Men should unbutton their jackets and sit on the tails to avoid making the jacket appear two sizes too big.

- Women should avoid wearing jangling, noisy bracelets and necklaces on radio or TV.

- Everyone should refrain from wearing shiny, sparkling jewels or highly polished silver or gold.

- If you normally wear eyeglasses, by all means, wear them during your interview as well.

● In short, do everything in your power to allow the focus of the interview to be on you, not your clothing or accessories.

Even if you're only being heard

A few words about dressing for radio interviews: Some guests assume that because the radio studio is absent of cameras, sloppy dress is acceptable. If a guest looks sloppy, the host has a hard time taking his or her views as seriously. Being well-groomed and dressing appropriately also adds to your self confidence, which comes across in your voice.

There are exceptions to every rule, of course. Motivator Dr. Wayne Dyer showed up for his *"Your Own Success"* interview wearing tennis shorts, a T-shirt and sneakers, and it turned out to be one of the best and most insightful shows we ever produced. It worked for him because his dress was consistent with the message he preaches: freedom, peace and comfort.

A helpful pre-interview checklist

So now you're dressed for success, and in reasonable control of your pre-show nerves. What else should you do, or prepare for, before the producer shouts, "Five seconds to air time?" Here's my list: Keep it handy.

1. Show up! You can do nothing worse than miss a scheduled interview. When you are booked, you become an integral part of that program. Other guests may be scheduled to compliment your talents and interests. Without you, a definite void *will* be noticeable. The host of the program may have "billboarded" your appearance on previous shows, and viewers or listeners may have arranged their schedules accordingly. The negative domino effect of missing an interview is immeasurable. And you will never be able to apologize enough. You will effectively end your talk show appearances prematurely. Of this you can be assured!

2. Show up *early,* at the very minimum 20 minutes before showtime. Pre-show activities may range from signing guest releases to spending a few minutes with a make-up man (if you're on TV) to briefing the host to just acclimating yourself to your environment.

3. If you want a copy of your TV interview, be sure you've made arrangements with friends to tape it for you. TV stations will not give you a tape of the show. You might, however, be able to purchase one, at cost. It's wise to have friends, family or associates tape the interview as a back-up plan. I'm always amazed by guests who overlook this obvious opportunity. The interview is not private– it is very, very public. Take advantage of that simple fact!

4. If you wish to have an audio copy of your radio interview, bring a blank cassette with you and ask the studio engineer to make an "air check." If the equipment is available, he will present you with a copy before you leave. Make sure that the tape is long enough for your interview.

Never ask for a copy of the interview *after* the fact! What may seem like a very simple request to you is actually a great inconvenience for the radio station. In order to accommodate your request, the master reel would have to be replayed and recorded on cassette.

5. Regardless of whether you already sent them to the station, remember to bring your prepared questions with you. You cannot depend on the producer to remember to discuss them with the host, or the host to read them. If you have a chance to meet with the host before the show, let him or her know that you have another copy of the questions if he or she needs them.

6. Ask for anything you'll need during the interview– water, pad, pencil– before the interview begins.

7. Be prepared to sign a guest release, if you haven't already done so.

Behind the scenes and studio hand signals

You may be curious about all the activity that precedes the show. By arriving early, you'll have a chance to witness some of this behind-the-scenes pandemonium, and discover that this seeming chaos is really the precise orchestration of several activities crucial to the smooth running of the show.

You may also want to familiarize yourself with the various hand signals that are used to communicate important information from the producer or stage manager to the host. Hand signals, rather than disruptive audible cues, are used to communicate to the host during live programming. Don't worry: You, as a guest, are not expected to know or respond to these signals.

However, I've noticed that some guests, especially those new to interviewing, tend to be thrown off track when hand signals are given. Perhaps they are feeling as though they are missing something. At any rate, I have witnessed more than one guest whose train of thought was broken by the flurry of hand signals passing back and forth.

Here are the most popular hand signals. Try practicing them at home so that you'll know what they feel and look like when you see them. You'll also be able to gauge your studio responses better by knowing what the host knows.

- **Pointing to a host:** The host should speak now! The microphone is open.

- **One, two, or three fingers held straight up:** Time remaining in minutes for this segment.

- **Pulling taffy motion:** Read or speak more slowly. Stretch— we need to fill time until the break or end of show.

- **Both hands rotating in a circular pedaling motion:** Speed up! Read or speak more rapidly, time is running out.

- **One hand rotating in a circular motion next to face:** Wrap it up! Bring the program to a fast close.

- **One or both hands are slowly raised, palm up:** Make the music or sound louder or speak up.

- **One or both hands are slowly lowered, palm down:** Make the music or sound softer or speak softer.

- **Index finger is drawn across the throat:** Cut! Stop the program, music or commercial ... now!

- **Clenched fist held sideways, thumb on top:** Only 30 seconds to go until the end of this segment (radio only).

In radio interviews, if listeners are invited to call in, you'll be given a set of headphones to hear their questions. Don't reject using the earphones. You can adjust them so that they are comfortable. Always ask where the volume control is located and use it if necessary. Don't become annoyed or fussy about messing your hair. Remember, you are on radio. No one but the host and staff can see you, and they are accustomed to wearing headphones and seeing guests wear them.

A few comments about ego

I have never witnessed another industry that seems to run on the collective egos of its members. Broadcast hosts and producers have gigantic egos. This is both good news and bad news. When you consider that hosts get "on camera" and "on microphone" every day and that, in so doing, they control a broadcast frequency that has the power to penetrate every living room, car and kitchen within a 50- to

100-mile radius, you begin to understand the need for a large ego. Producers and hosts of talk shows couldn't survive in this cutthroat industry if they had lightweight egos. The bad news is that sometimes they clash with the large egos of guests who also feel very powerful.

I have never seen a guest win an ego war with a producer or host of a talk show. This may not sound like fair play. But that's the way it is.

I recall an unfortunate incident that occurred on a friend's radio talk show. She was about to conduct a telephone interview with a guest, the author of a marketing book called ***How to Make Clients Your Friends*** or something like that. Things were hectic in the show schedule that day, necessitating putting the guest on hold for about 20 minutes. Finally, when the guest was introduced, all of New York heard her sarcastic response, "I can't believe you put me on hold for all that time. I've never been treated like this. It's about time I'm on the air. Now let's talk about ***How to Make Clients Your Friends.***"

At that point, my friend ended the interview by pushing the button and saying, "I'd love to have that conversation when you learn how to do it yourself. Let's go to a break..." This author's uncontrollable ego not only got in the way of a free and potentially productive interview, but actually damaged her credibility and certainly sold no books that day.

If you have a chance to meet the host prior to the show, you can take advantage of this opportunity to initiate a positive working relationship. By working *with* your host, you'll be able to take advantage of his or her skill and expertise to make your interview a successful experience for you.

Talk show guests' Bill of Rights

Unfortunately, the glacial ego of a talk show host is sometimes the tip of the iceberg that signals cold-hearted treatment of guests. I firmly believe that a certain courteous and professional attitude must always be extended to each guest– by each and every broadcast station, no matter how big or small. Unfortunately, some violators tend to be larger market stations, where cooler heads and attitudes should prevail. Whatever the reasons, as a media consultant, I have heard enough complaints by my clients to justify writing the following Bill of Rights to caution them and the readers of **On The Air** against further indignities.

The following are the *minimum* standards that guests should accept. Any behavior not in accordance with these standards warrants complaint to station management.

1. Talk show guests have the right to be treated in a friendly, courteous, professional manner prior to, during, and after the radio or television interview.

2. Talk show guests have the right to receive an explanation of the program workings and equipment, such as microphones and headphones, that they will use.

3. Talk show guests have the right to request and receive simple amenities– a glass of water, pencil or writing pad.

4. Talk show guests have the right to know the identity of all other guests who will be appearing within the same segment.

5. Talk show guests have the right to an explanation of all visual cues before the actual broadcast.

6. Talk show guests have the right to request and receive the actual air date for any taped shows in which they will appear.

7. TV talk show guests have the right to determine the wording of any superimposed identity graphic that will appear on the air during the interview.

8. TV talk show guests have the right to view themselves on a studio monitor on a fully lit set prior to the interview.

9. TV talk show guests have the right to request that studio lights be turned off or dimmed during commercial and other breaks.

10. TV talk show guests have the right to be seated in a lighted set no more than five minutes before taping begins.

11. TV talk show guests have the right to rehearse any visual props for appropriate camera angles with appropriate professional suggestions from director or stage manager.

Chapter 6

You're On!

Your big moment is finally here. Your notes are in hand. Your water glass is filled. Pad and pencil are placed before you. The microphone is attached, and your host is introducing you to an audience of potential customers, clients or readers. You've got your limelight jitters under control, and you're ready to roll. It is at this important moment that all your careful preparations should pay off. You've thought of everything.

Haven't you?

Here are some final pointers, hints and information to ensure that your interview experience will be a successful one.

Your host, your captain

Rely on your host to guide you, comfortably and safely, through your interview. He is, indeed, the captain of his ship. He has navigated the waters, he has charted the course, and he knows better than anyone where his ship is headed. Allow him to *be* the captain. He may want to take the conversation on a course that seems illogical to you, but don't stop him. He knows what he's doing.

Focus on the interview

Don't let the microphones, news wire machines, telephone calls, and general frenzied environment of the radio station throw you. Nothing is more embarrassing and more damaging than to find yourself lost in the conversation and struggling to keep up. This won't happen if you keep focused.

Astronaut Wally Schirra almost panicked during our *"Your Own Success"* interview when a news alert came in as he was speaking. He lost his train of thought as the bright red light began to blink. "Where I come from, blinking red lights mean big trouble," he said as he struggled to get back on track (and did so with style). Try not to let outside annoyances interrupt your thinking process.

Talk, don't read

Don't depend on your notes for your responses. Time has proven that the best guests are those who can think on their feet, listen attentively and provide seemingly spontaneous answers. If you are *over*prepared, you may come across as *under*prepared and phony. I am conditioned to worry if, before an interview, a guest begins to assemble neat piles of paper. I just know that it won't be a great interview.

Expletives avoided

Assume that your microphone is on at all times. Don't make the mistake of talking to the host as you head to a commercial break, or swearing in relief when you think you're off the air. Most radio studios have a red "on air" light, which is illuminated automatically if a studio microphone is "hot" or turned on. *Wait until the light goes off, even if you hear a commercial, before you speak.*

I've been very lucky in the five years we've been doing *"Your Own Success."* We've only experienced one profanity incident. Most live shows, both radio and television, are on a seven-second time delay. Both the host and the producer have a "dump button." By pushing it, everything that is said up to seven seconds earlier is, literally, "dumped" before hitting the air.

And now, a word from our sponsor

Never, *never* interfere with a commercial break, or make light of an advertiser. Don't try to make a point while the host is attempting to go to a commercial. The host is trained to pace the show. Take his lead when he cuts you off and says something like, "Tell us about that when we come back from this break."

Commercials are the lifeblood of broadcasting. A true business definition of a radio or TV show is a series of costly and precisely scheduled commercials into which program material is cleverly interwoven in such a way as to highlight each commercial. The host knows, when he cuts for a commercial, that it is *these* breaks, which may seem disruptive to you, that pay his salary, the salaries of the camera crew, the producer and the general overhead.

I will never forget an incident at my first broadcasting job. I was in the affiliate relations department of ABC television when we received word that lightning had interrupted programming at an affiliate station in West Virginia. My boss told me to find out "exactly what did not get on the air." I saw this as a golden opportunity to show my stuff. I called the station and found out that the long-running soap opera, "All My Children," had been interrupted. I determined the timing of the outage and immediately telephoned the programming department to learn how much of the story had been lost. I assembled all this information, including all missed dialogue from the script, and proudly dumped it on my boss's desk.

His response taught me an invaluable and unforgettable lesson in broadcast priorities. He glanced at my report, looked up at me and growled, "What is this garbage? Where are the commercials? What *commercials* are missing? Who cares about the damn *program!*"

Turn dumb questions into smart responses

You may be asked a question that you simply don't want to get stuck answering. It could be a volatile issue that could ignite negative response, or a personal one that makes you uncomfortable. Many times, however, it will just be an irrelevant question that wastes valuable time.

There is a secret to handling these moments– I call it the "Reagan flip." When then-President Reagan was asked a question he didn't wish to answer, he frequently responded to a question that he wished someone *had* asked. No wonder he was called the Great Communicator!

Orson Bean elaborates on the "Reagan flip." "When you are asked a dumb or boring question, change it to an interesting one and answer that." If you handle this adroitly, he explains, the interviewer and the audience will not even notice what you have done: "When the question you don't want to answer is asked, you respond, 'It's interesting that you should ask that because only yesterday I was saying to myself'...and you go on from there."

As an example, if an interviewer asks him whether he prefers stage or film work, he might reply, "It's funny you should ask that because only this morning I happened to remember the time when I was working in the theater with Jayne Mansfield and her bra fell off..."

He continues, "Compliment [the interviewer] on the question and then change it to the one you wish he'd asked. In my experience, no interviewer has ever realized what I was doing. They are only grateful that I've been a good interview."

Be prepared for anything

When something unplanned occurs during your talk show interview, the way in which you choose to react has everything to do with the successful outcome. Read through these nightmare stories and ponder how *you* would have acted if the same thing had happened to you:

- Robert Ringer, author of the best-selling books **Winning Through Intimidation** and **Looking Out For #1**, relayed this live TV horror story to me. "Without advance notice or warning of any kind, Vidal Sassoon plopped a woman's blond wig on my head and asked me how an intimidator like me would handle the situation. The cameras zoomed in and captured my frozen, stunned expression, bleached blond wig and all, in all its splendor. Vidal lived– barely."

- Entrepreneur Mikki Williams was the subject in a segment of a *Lifetime* cable program: "They taped a microphone to my dress. The weight pulled the front of my dress down and the heat of the lights made me sweat and dislodged the tape. I have a videotape of myself glancing down to see how far the neckline was dragging, then a jerky motion and a pained expression on my face when it fell."

- Sometimes other guests do the unexpected at your expense. "My first TV experience," recalls Warren Greshes, motivational speaker, "had John Molloy, author of **Dress For Success**, on before me. He stated that 'paisley ties were out.' Naturally, that's exactly what I was wearing." Greshes saved the moment by announcing that he was burning his tie as he walked out after his introduction.

- Brain surgeon Dr. Vernon Mark went on an unexpected ride of his life during a recent TV talk show. "I was seated on a moving TV stage that was pushed so hard that it went right past the TV cameras and crashed into the opposite wall."

- Husband-and-wife team Jane and Robert Handly lecture about overcoming life's challenges and have appeared on major shows including *"Donahue,"*and *"Nightline"*, were invited to be the sole guests on a one-hour Christian radio show. Only one problem: The host didn't show up. The resourceful team had the perfect solution– "We went on the air and interviewed each other," said Bob. "It went really well."

● Ron Rotstein, a futurist, was asked, what the future of ladies underwear was likely to be by a serious radio caller.

● Roger Herman was being interviewed on an Atlanta radio talk show when telephone difficulties took over. "We were getting partial questions. The engineer even had to recall me several times. For two hours, we shifted from taking calls to one-on-one conversation. We'd get started talking about something, cut it off to take a call or two, then start a conversation again. Interesting night!" sums up Herman.

● Sometimes hosts can be just as astonishing in their behavior. Roger Dawson was waiting to be introduced on a radio talk show in Adelaide, Australia. The host said, "I really don't agree with this next piece at all, but my producer talked me into doing it. There's another American motivator coming through town doing a seminar. I don't agree with it, but here's Roger Dawson. Now Roger, you don't really believe this stuff works, do you?" "And it went downhill from there," reported Dawson.

● Sometimes hosts just don't do their homework. This story was relayed to me by seminar leader Barbara Abrams Mintzer: "I was on a radio show and suddenly I was asked to explain how the concept of Jesus Christ fit into my life. Being a

Jewish girl from Brooklyn, this really had no pertinent meaning in my life. However, I gave some 'spiritual' answer that I think went over fairly well. This was an example of a host who did not take the time out to find out who his guests were before the show went on the air," said Mintzer.

Rules for radio telephone interviews

The majority of radio interviews are conducted by telephone, and most of these are conducted live. The state-of-the-art equipment in radio stations can enhance the ordinary sound of the telephone so that listeners can't tell that you're not in the studio. In most cases, the studio will arrange to call you for the interview at a predetermined time. During commercials the host will put your call on hold. When he does so, you will be able to hear the commercial messages through your telephone. He will then reintroduce you and "punch you up" on the air again. The conversation will pick up from where it left off. Sometimes a host will "pick you up" during the commercial to compare notes and guide the conversation. (You are not on the air at this point, so don't panic.)

Here are steps you should follow to maximize the sound quality of your telephone interview:

1. Be sure you've given the studio the number of a telephone that is located in a quiet room. Don't use a telephone located in a high-traffic area of your home or near crying babies or barking dogs.

2. Never do an interview from a cellular telephone, especially in a moving vehicle. As your car moves, a loud clicking sound will be heard as your system switches into different cells. Many times, especially in larger cities with tall buildings, switching cells will disconnect the call.

3. Don't arrange to conduct your interview from a telephone with a call-waiting feature. If you are called by someone else during the interview, the call waiting signal will be disruptive to listeners. If you have no choice, call all those people who are apt to call you, and tell them *not* to call during the interview. If you are signalled by your call-waiting feature during your interview, do nothing and say nothing about the interference. The host may wish to make a light comment about your popularity.

4. Make sure you are by the phone and ready to pick it up when the producer calls. Sometimes the show is running a little late. The producer will usually call you at the appointed time, just to let you know how long a delay to expect.

5. Don't keep the radio station tuned in during your interview. The station is programming on a seven-second delay. You'll drive yourself crazy if you attempt to listen to your radio while you're being interviewed.

6. Don't have someone listen to your interview by picking up on another extension. This will lower the quality and clarity of the sound, especially on lesser-quality telephones. If the telephone quality is bad, the studio engineer will convey this information to the host, and your interview may be jeopardized or shortened.

7. If you have another telephone in the room in which you are going to be interviewed, mention this to the producer. Ask that the studio or a friend call the other number to render it inactive. Just answer it, and put the receiver aside until after the interview. By doing this, you will avoid the other line ringing loudly in the same room while you are conducting your interview.

8. Never refer to a bad-quality line, crackling, or other audio problems while on air. The sounds may not be heard by the studio or the listeners. If there is a problem, the host will say something and instruct the engineer to call you back either on air or during a commercial break. If the noise is too distracting to you and the studio is not aware of it, mention it only while talking to the host or producer during the commercial break. The filtering equipment at most radio stations is capable of eliminating distracting noises during the call.

9. If you don't receive the studio call at the appointed time, always have the studio telephone number nearby and call them. This call can save your interview if they have an incorrect number. They may also have had a difficult time in reaching you for various technical reasons. Most likely, however, they're just running late and have not gotten around to making a courtesy call to alert you to the time change for your interview.

Taped interviews

The words "taped show" should immediately get your adrenalin flowing, because *only taped programs offer the potential of being repeated,* sometimes several times. Think about the added value of a great interview being replayed. If it performed well for you the first time, you can certainly expect a good response the second or third time around.

The best thing about these repeat performances? No effort on your part is necessary. Your telephone will ring with qualified potential customers, and it's all a bonus.

If you're scheduled for a taped interview, do everything in your power to maintain its "evergreen," or timeless, nature: Avoid saying anything that will prematurely age the program. Don't refer to the time of day, even by saying "good morning" or "good afternoon." Instead, say "hello," and "good bye." Avoid extending seasonal greetings, or referring to the time of year. And don't comment on the weather. Any of these references can prematurely age the taped program.

In general, the taped interview has a significantly less frenzied pace than a live one. So you'll have more opportunity to concentrate on your "evergreen" phrasing.

Chapter 7

After Your First Interview: More Is Best!

Whew! You made it through the interview. You were eloquent, witty, entertaining and, if you do say so yourself, the perfect guest. Not only that, your appearance has already generated a terrific response! You can consider your hard work and efforts a great success. Your job is over, right?

Wrong!

Most novice guests cut their learning curve– and their talk show potential– short. While you may have achieved your goal of pulling off a business-generating interview, you can make that experience continue to work for you. You have a new goal now– to get invited back.

Any producer with an eye for excellence will keep a hot list of versatile guests who have performed well and are worth repeating. When I appeared on a segment of the *"Morton Downey Jr. Show,"* I argued that colleges were turning out mediocre graduates. My opposition was an out-spoken Midwestern college professor. To my amazement, I learned during the pre-show briefing that this professor was making his sixth appearance on the show because "he really knows how to elicit a riotous studio audience." (If I ever have the privilege of meeting you in person, I'll fill you in on the outcome of that confrontation.)

Keep in mind that producers will *not* book you again immediately, no matter *how* good you were. They desire a constant flow of fresh faces and diverse opinions. But by following up effectively, you'll secure a place on the producer's list of tried-and-true call-backs, and you may eventually make a repeat performance.

Follow-up strategies for getting invited back

As a producer, I've observed a definite lack of follow up from guests and their public-relations people. This is proof in itself that most guests see their talk show activity as only a temporary part of their larger marketing plan. When you finish an interview, you have a perfect opportunity to request another one, especially if the experience was a good one, or if you felt that there was more to say and not enough time to say it. Here are some key strategies that should always follow up a good interview.

1. Send personal thank-you notes to the producer and the host of the program. Using stationery or postcards that have your picture is a plus. Hosts and producers meet thousands of people each year. You must attempt to stand out if you expect to be invited back. If sending a thank-you note seems "obvious," then why have I only received *10* thank-you notes from the *2,500* guests I've interviewed over the years? I've saved all of them, because of their oddity value and to prove my point. Three of these 10 savvy guests have appeared again on our show.

2. If your appearance was covered in any print media, send copies of the write-up to the producer and host, attaching a personal note mentioning that you'd like to be invited back. This is just one more way to stay in touch. You would be surprised at how appreciated this effort is. Hosts and producers often don't get a chance to see anything more then the barrage of guests who zoom in and out of the studio as if on a fast-moving conveyor belt. When you send along an article featuring your appearance on their show, you can't help but stand apart from other guests.

Additionally, the station sales staff will use this type of article to show potential advertisers. The station's public relations department will want a copy as well for its public service file. Make sure to mention these uses to the producer and host, and send extra copies for internal departments.

3. Approximately 30 days after your interview, send a letter, separate and apart from the thank-you notes and articles. In this letter, remind the producer who you are, and mention how well your original interview was received. You can then introduce new ideas, new hooks and new slants for a future interview.

Keep sending these reminder letters every 30 to 60 days. Be sure to mention new projects, send along new articles you've written or in which you've appeared, or send any new products or product descriptions, audios, videos or books. Every six months, send your complete and updated media kit.

4. Add the names of the producer and host to your mailing list, whether you regularly mail press releases, a newsletter or holiday cards.

5. Volunteer your services as a standby guest. This is a most powerful strategy– one that rarely occurs to would-be guests. Simply inform the producer that you can be available at a moment's notice in the event that a scheduled guest cancels.

Give the producer all your private telephone numbers– including your mother's number, your sister's number, your next door neighbor's number, your car phone, the weekend house, and the number of anyone who can track you down in case of a no-show. Put all these telephone numbers on an index card with your name, address, and topics of expertise. On the top of the card, print the words "Emergency Guest" underscored in red. At the conclusion of every outstanding television or radio interview in which you've participated, hand this prepared card to the producer. Inform him or her, with as much excitement as you can muster, that you can be trusted to go the extra mile to solve any future guest problems they may experience.

Only three people have made such an offer to me, and I have tracked them down, called and re-interviewed all of them in emergency situations. Every producer will ultimately need the service of a standby guest– it makes sense for the producer to call upon a tried-and-true guest.

Springboarding to other talk shows

Now you're a proven commodity. You'll find that your first talk show appearance gives you credibility with other talk show producers. You can use some of the same strategies you'd use for getting invited back to leverage other appearances, as well. In addition, you'll want to send a videotape of your appearance to other producers. Videotapes are very easy and inexpensive to duplicate today– just look in the yellow pages under "Television Production" or "Post-Production Facilities."

As you land more interviews– and your reputation as a crowd-pleasing guest grows– you may start to receive unsolicited invitations to appear on talk shows! While I certainly wish you the inconvenience of having your phone ringing off the hook with such offers, I do offer some advice: Don't do every interview that comes along. There will come a time when you should become a bit choosy about how you spend your time interviewing.

You *should* do every interview offered to you at the beginning of your learning curve, even if it's only to practice your style and get a little more comfortable with radio and television interviews. After a while, however, you should focus on talk show programs on stations in the top 100 markets, then the top 50 markets (see Chapter 2, as well as the Databanks at the end of this book).

I know some guests who will only do national and top-10 market shows. Why? As we've discussed, it all boils down to numbers. You have to work just as hard and invest just as much time in every interview you do. So, you might as well concentrate on markets the size of Chicago or New York City that will deliver audiences of more than one million.

Furthermore, you won't even want to do every interview in the *top* markets that comes along. A particular major-market program may attract an audience that would not be interested in your topic. Everyone, for example, would seemingly love to appear on the "biggies"– *"The Tonight Show," "Phil Donahue,"* etc.

If you are a management consultant, should you spend *your* time trying to land such an appearance? *"The Tonight Show"* has a heavy entertainment format with little social comment or hard information. *"Phil Donahue,"* on the other hand, deals with social problems and topical headline news, with few exceptions. For the most part, these shows deliver radically *different* audiences, yet a discussion of your management consulting work would be lost on *both* of them.

While both are top-rated programs, neither would do much to help your publicity needs. Presuming you actually could convince the producer of either to put you on (a long-shot, given your topic), you would simply confuse and annoy their audiences.

So, obviously, your time *shouldn't* be devoted to landing interviews on such shows.

Make sure you do a similar audience and format analysis of the shows you think you want to go after...before you waste your time on "big" shows that are completely wrong for your business, book, product or cause.

Ready for a media tour?

When your talk show invitations begin to increase, you may want to think in terms of planning a media tour. Be prepared for a hectic pace, a commitment of personal time and a financial investment– flights and hotel rooms add up. If you have a large budget, but want to avoid the hassles and aggravation of the travel schedule, you should investigate a satellite media tour. This enables you to appear on several local television stations nationwide– while actually only taping your interviews in a single studio. All travel and associated costs and aggravation is eliminated.

How does it work? A satellite tour company, in a sense, is your publicist. It offers topic consultations, plans bookings and offers studio facilities to tape your interview.

A major provider of this service is Media Link's Video Public Relations Network. According to the brochures, a guest can actually do 25 home-based TV interviews by satellite to 25 separate cities, in four hours. The cost starts at about $9,000 and covers topic consultation, station bookings, studio facilities and satellite time, plus technical coordination and usage monitoring. (Media Link, 708 Third Avenue, New York, NY 10017; 212-682-8300.)

Other satellite tour companies include: J-Nex Satellite Services (5455 Wilshire Blvd., Los Angeles, CA 90036; 213-934-4356) and Orbis Productions (3322 North Lakewood Ave., Chicago, IL 60657; 312-883-9584).

Advertising: Stretch your interview impact

We've already reviewed the advantages of the talk show *interview* as opposed to the talk show *commercial* (Introduction): First, it's free, and second, the editorial portion of a program is often perceived as having more credibility than the advertising segments. Nevertheless, I recommend exploring advertising on the very show that you've appeared on. Yes, commercials cost money. But if you do it right, you may discover that you've doubled the impact of your message– and enhanced your business.

Regarding *radio* talk show advertising, however, you must understand this important fact: Radio advertising can be a great targeted lead generator, but it is *not* an effective one-step sales generator, particularly for high-ticket items. Most people won't send large checks or give their credit card numbers after just *hearing about* a product or service, and not actually seeing them demonstrated. You'll have to use a *two*-step sales program: Generate the interest, or lead, *then* sell via follow-up marketing material, brochures and/or a sales call.

Advice on producing your commercial

If you do plan to advertise, here are some tips to make your ads more effective:

- Use a local telephone number or an 800 number (unless, of course, you're selling a 900 telephone number or similar service).
- Mention the telephone number three times during the commercial.
- Don't mention the telephone number in the first two-thirds of the script.
- Be sure to mention the telephone number immediately before closing the commercial.
- Don't ask listeners to write for information. Most will not.
- Only sell through the commercial if the product or service is valued under $20. Otherwise, use the two-step approach.
- Use 60-second spots, not 30's, *never* 15's.
- Ask the station to produce the spot at no charge to you, using station talent, music and effects.
- Insist that at least some of your spots be placed in the most popular programs in drive time (6 a.m. to 10 a.m, 3 p.m. to 7 p.m.). Remember, this is the time when the listening audience is the largest.

Air your commercial– without paying a dime

Some talk show guests forget that the business in which they're engaged can lend itself to other outstanding possibilities with the very stations on which they appear as guests. You can negotiate a barter or trade arrangement with most radio stations and some TV stations.

Radio stations are in the unique position of hardly ever paying cash for their needs. They don't have to– they have all that in-demand advertising time available to the highest bidder. At 16 minutes per hour, radio stations have up to 384 minutes to sell *every day of the year*. The most popular time is usually always sold– the commercial minutes between 6 am and 7 pm. But the bulk of the remaining time– some of which is excellent, most of which is good to mediocre– is usually available at discount or held for trade.

Let's say you are a sales trainer. You can call the sales manager of the station to alert him to your upcoming interview. Ask that he listen in as you are interviewed. After your appearance, assuming you've impressed him with your knowledge, you can offer to train the members of the station sales staff in exchange for advertising time on the station. You can then use the advertising time to sell your services as a sales trainer or, perhaps, to sell or give away tickets to an upcoming introductory seminar to business people in the listening area.

Try to negotiate a four-, three- or two-to-one deal. That is, you'll give the station $1,000 worth of your training services or products in exchange for $4,000, $3,000 or $2,000 worth of advertising time on the radio station. In all cases, be sure that the advertising rate quoted to you is consistent with the station's advertising rate card.

If you're considering proposing a trade agreement with a television station, be aware that they have less commercial inventory with which to trade than radio stations, so they are less apt to enter into such an agreement. Television advertising is much more expensive– most stations reach a much greater audience than radio. TV spots are usually 30 seconds in length, radio commercials generally 60. Lastly, TV commercials are expensive to produce and, therefore, are most often *not* given gratis to buyers of advertising.

Even with all these negatives, it's still worth trying to arrange a trade deal with TV stations on which you're appearing as a guest. A well-produced TV commercial running consistently on a good station can increase your business– fast.

Chapter 8

Wisdom

Of

The Experts

You now have all the secrets that a very small minority of talk show guests have been keeping to themselves. You also have a chronological plan with a beginning, middle and successful conclusion. You possess a special insight now, because you know how producers and hosts think, and how they get the job done. You understand the restraints and the behind-the-scenes pressures. You are also aware of the post-interview opportunities.

Now that you've learned to traverse this sometimes unsettling terrain, it's just about time to issue a roadmap to plan your trip, one that will ensure that you'll know where you're headed at all times. The last part of this book– the Databanks– include listings of talk-formatted radio and TV programs as well as market-by-market breakdowns of radio and television stations nationwide (including Canadian markets) that are seeking guests for locally produced talk shows.

However, before we conclude, there is one more component I want to share with you, a gift to boost your confidence: Advice from the pros. I asked friends and associates interviewed on *"Your Own Success"* for the one piece of advice that would comfort and support someone new to talk shows. There's great power in squeezing years of experience into one brief comment. What results, as you will see...is wisdom!

- "Stay loose. Keep your answers short. Maintain a sense of humor, relax and enjoy it."
  Al Neuharth

- "Know your subject, respect your interviewer, make the uninteresting, interesting."
  Stan Katz

- "Take control of the interview. Give short punchy answers (like this!)."
  Roger Dawson

- "Don't take yourself too seriously. Smile. Stay loose. The world's existence does not depend on your being a charming guest on this particular show. Relax...you'll do a much better job"
  Og Mandino

- "Be yourself, be prepared and enjoy the process."
  Fred Pryor

- "Don't overprepare. Be yourself. Don't worry about mistakes. They make good television and radio."
  David Brown

- "Give strong opinions and stay away from yes or no answers and occasionally say something reasonably outrageous (if you believe it)."
  Art Linkletter

● "No matter what you expect or how much you prepare, always be prepared for the unexpected."
Skip Cypert

● "Relax, since that advice probably won't be taken, the second is...Practice on videotape (even for radio) many times."
Bert Decker

● "Forget the glitz; eliminate the vanity; Don't try to be 'showbiz.' Be honest, get into the content of your subject. People aren't too interested in you. They want to know what you can do for them."
Robert J. Ringer

● "Forget the mike and the camera. Give yourself the mindset that you're talking to one interested person only...not the whole world."
Barbara Brabec

● "Relax and realize that most hosts are smart enough to want to make you sound and look good, because if you look good, they look good."
Michael LeBoeuf

● "Be quotable. Have your 'lines' down. Realize that you are the entertainment and need to put on a good show. Be outspoken."
Jimmy Calano

● "Be enthusiastic, be authentic, be honest. Talk as if you are in your living room, rather than participating in an interview."
Dr. Wayne Dyer

● "Relax! You wouldn't be here if you weren't an expert in your area. Loosen your tie (radio) and be human. Don't worry about saying something dumb. Have fun. It's your 15 minutes, in Andy Warhol's words. Might as well enjoy them."

Tom Peters

● "Rehearse ... then converse!"

Dr. Gilda Carle

● "Pour on the enthusiasm! It takes money to buy, but enthusiasm to sell."

Stew Leonard

● "Practice your one liners."

Joe Mancuso

● "Use as many crutches as the interviewer uses."

Carole Hyatt

● "Know that your information is valuable. Speak with commitment. Do not be afraid to promote yourself or the value of your product or service."

Austin McGonigle

● "Get as much in touch as you can with the vibrations and nuances of the interviewer. Work together and truly listen to your interviewer. He is not an adversary and can be your partner in getting your point across."

Richard Lederer

● "Know your subject well. Then tell the truth as you see it. Think of helping the viewers and listeners and not trying to make yourself look good."

Gil Eagles

● "Don't be apologetic about your convictions. Keep the whine out of your voice– ie., say it with power!"
Alan Cox

● "Use examples and if possible, some humor directly relevant to your point. Forget the fact that there is an audience. Just have a friendly conversation."
John Diebold

● "Think about the primary purpose (ie. to sell books). Think ahead of time about three key points you want to make and weave them in no matter what the host asks."
Warren Bennis

● "Don't assume that the interviewer knows what is the most important idea or information you have to offer. They don't."
Dr. Lane Longfellow

● "Be natural– while you may want to be 'perfect,' the audience wants to see or hear you natural. If you screw up, laugh. Don't beat yourself up."
Ted Dreier

● "Never be boring"
Dorothy Leeds

● "Talk shows represent the great untapped marketing tool of the '90s. If you are not participating in this free giveaway, get started today! You now know how."
Al Parinello

Epilogue

An Important Final Word Before You Begin

Life offers us very few truly unforgettable experiences. I feel blessed that I've actually been able to meet and befriend most of my heroes and mentors. One was the great motivator, broadcaster and audiocassette entrepreneur, the late Earl Nightingale.

We had a few minutes alone, getting acquainted before our *"Your Own Success"* interview in 1987. Suddenly Earl stopped, shook his head and stared at the microphone. Softly, he whispered, "I still can't believe it, I still can't get over it. All you have to do is talk into that thing and you profoundly affect hundreds of thousands– if not millions– of lives. What a responsibility. What a privilege!"

It was a powerful moment. This coming from a man who's been behind the microphone for more than 40 years.

Above everything you've learned here, please recognize this responsibility. Television and radio are perceived to be bigger than life. People trust what they see and hear. With your media appearance, you can and will change lives. Make a commitment to change those lives...for the better.

As Earl said, "What a privilege!"

Happy interviews!

Databanks

Helpful Information To Get You Started

Following is a compilation of industry information that you will not find anywhere else. I've gathered an extensive list of both radio and TV talk shows, as well as addresses, phone and FAX numbers of hundreds of radio and TV stations throughout the United States and Canada. Keep this as your "yellow pages" for researching interview opportunities. As you read through this section, you may want to review Chapter 2 as well.

As we've already discussed, the broadcast industry is constantly changing. Thus, while these comprehensive Databanks are current as of presstime, this information is indeed subject to change.

If you're interested in getting a more specific list of local talk shows, including names and phone numbers of the producers, please don't hesitate to contact me at: American Media Ventures, P.O. Box 279, Norwood, N.J. 07648, (201) 784-0059.

Databank 1

Television
Talk Shows

A: Television Network Programs

The following is a listing of major television network talk shows that require guests and feature a variety of toopics. Some networks are not included (such as Fox) because they are not currently programming talk shows. Some popular talk-formatted shows are excluded because they do not interview guests except for major celebrities.

**ABC TV: American
Broadcasting Company**

Talk Shows:
Good Morning America
1965 Broadway
New York, NY 10023-5904
(212) 496-4800
(212) 456-4724 (FAX)

The Health Show
ABC-TV
1717 DeSales Street NW
Washington, DC 20036-4407
(202) 887-7963
(202) 887-7790 (FAX)

Nightline
ABC News
1717 DeSales Street NW
Washington DC 20036-4407
(202) 877-7360

Prime Time Live
ABC News
1965 Broadway, 4th Floor
New York, New York 10023
(212) 580-6186

CBS TV: Columbia Broadcasting System

Talk Shows:
CBS This Morning
524 West 57th Street
New York, NY 10019-2985
(212) 975-2824
(212) 975-2115 (FAX)

CBS Morning News
(same address)
(212) 975-4321

Face The Nation
CBS - TV
2020 M Street NW
Washington DC 20036
(202) 457-4481

Night Watch
CBS-TV
2033 M Street NW #201
Washington DC 20036-3305
(202) 775-6854

This Morning's Business
Financial News Network
1251 Avenue of the Americas
New York, NY 10020
(212) 827-0071

No Listing in NYC

N/A

NBC TV: National Broadcasting Corporation

Talk Shows:
Today Show
NBC-TV
30 Rockefeller Plaza #304
New York, NY 10112-0317
(212) 664-4249

Sunday Today
(same address)
(212) 664-2937

The Tonight Show Starring Johnny Carson
NBC-TV
3000 W. Alameda Avenue
Burbank, CA 91523-0001
(818) 840-3682

Late Night With David Letterman
NBC-TV
30 Rockefeller Plaza
New York, NY 10112-0317
(212) 664-5907

Later With Bob Costas
NBC-TV
888 Seventh Avenue, 30th Floor
New York, NY 10106
(212) 399-1400

Meet The Press
NBC-TV
4001 Nebraska Avenue NW
Washington, DC 20016-2733
(202) 885-4598

PBS: Public Broadcasting Service

Talk Shows:
Adam Smith's Money World
Alvin H. Perlmuter
Corporation
45 West 45th Street, 15th Floor
New York, NY 10036-1896
(212) 221-6310

Firing Line
PBS-TV
150 East 35th Street
New York, NY 10016-4178
(212) 679-7330
(212) 696-0309 (FAX)

Nightly Business Report
WPBT-TV
14901 NE 20th
Miami, Florida 33181
(305) 949-8321
 (305) 949-9772 (FAX)

The McLaughlin Group/
McLaughlin One-on-One
1211 Connecticut Ave. NW #810
Washington, DC 20036
(202) 457-0870
(202)296-2285 (FAX)

Wall Street Week
WMPB-TV
11767 Bonita Avenue
Owings Mills, MD 21117-1414
4/0(301) 356-5600
(301)581-4338/04 (FAX)

N/A Rich Dubroff

B: Syndicated Television Talk Shows

These television programs are syndicated to broadcast TV stations on a market-by-market basis.

The Arsenio Hall Show
Paramount Television
5555 Melrose Avenue
Los Angeles, CA 90038-3197
(213) 468-3740

Live With Regis and Kathie Lee
WABC-TV
7 Lincoln Square, 5th Floor
New York, NY 10023-5906
(212) 887-3054
(212) 496-5249 (FAX)

Geraldo Rivera Show
Investigative News Group
311 West 43rd Street,
Penthouse
New York, NY 10036-6413
(212) 265-8520
(212) 581-8196 (FAX)

The Oprah Winfrey Show
HARPO, Inc.
P.O. Box 067640
Chicago, IL 60606-7640
(312) 591-9595

The Joan Rivers Show
524 West 57th Street
New York, NY 10019-2985
(212) 975-5522

The Phil Donahue Show
30 Rockefeller Plaza
New York, NY 10112-0317
(212) 664-6501
(212) 757-5386 (FAX)

Sally Jessy Raphael Show
510 West 57th Street
New York, NY 10019
(212) 582-1722

PM Magazine
Group W
825 Battery Street
San Francisco, CA 94111
(415) 362-4759
(415) 362-4756 (FAX)

**Steve Crowley's Money Pro/
The American Scene**
5100 NW 33rd Street
Fort Lauderdale, FL 33309
(305) 735-5222
(305) 735-5226 (FAX)

DeCesare, Dino

The Home Show
Woody Fraser Productions
4151 Prospect Avenue
Hollywood, CA 90027
(213) 557-4011
(213) 663-2583 (FAX)

The Marsha Warfield Show
Kline & Friends Inc.
12711 Ventura Boulevard
Studio City, CA 91604
(818) 985-1004

Family NIWS/MED NIWS
NIWS Productions
5432 West 102nd Street
Los Angeles, CA 90045
(213) 337-3382

Evening Magazine
Group W
855 Battery Street
San Francisco, CA 94111-1597
(415) 765-8820

**Fight Back! with David
Horowitz**
KNBC-TV
3000 West Alameda
Burbank, CA 91523-0001
(818) 840-4444

First Business
Biznet
1615 H Street NW
Washington DC 20062
(202) 463-5928

Jay Garfinkel

Health Matters/Med*Source
Medstar Communications
5920 Hamilton Boulevard
Allentown, PA 18016
(215) 395-1300
(215) 391-1556 (FAX)

Mind Your Business *No Listing in Sarasota*
VideoRap Productions
1540 N. Lockwood Ridge,. #230
Sarasota, FL 33577
(813) 366-1784 *(921-3139) N/A*

Viewpoint on Nutrition
708 Katherine Drive
Montebello, CA 90640-2751
(213) 723-1516

Wall Street Journal Report
Wall Street Journal Television
200 Liberty Street
New York, NY 10281
(212) 416-2000
(212) 416-3299 (FAX)

Ken Witty

Wally George Show
KDOC-TV
P.O. Box 787
Hollywood, CA 90028
(818) 906-0860

World of Travel
Studio M Productions
8715 Waikiki Station
Honolulu, HI 96815
(808) 734-3345

**Everyday With Joan
Lunden**
Michael Krauss Productions
707 Westchester Avenue
White Plains, NY 10604
(914) 761-9790
(914) 761-4015 (FAX)

America's Black Forum
2016 "O" Street NW
Washington, DC 20036
(202) 833-3915
(202) 296-7908 (FAX)

Bookmark Show
Compass Films
666 Broadway, 2nd Floor
New York, NY 10012
(212) 473-2230
(212) 473-4295

**Connie Martinson Talks
Books**
LaSalle Productions
2288 Cold Water Canyon
Beverly Hills, CA 90210-1756
(213) 271-4127

**Cookin' Round The
Country**
P.O. Box 907
46A Main Street
Tiburnon, CA 94920
(415) 383-6585

Ebony/Jet Showcase
Ebony/Jet Magazines
820 South Michigan
Chicago, IL 60611
(312) 322-9420
(312) 322-0918

C: Superstation Programs

These are independent local TV stations distributed by satellite to cable television systems nationwide. Thus, it's possible to see an Atlanta station in Los Angeles. This exposure makes talk show efforts on superstations as valuable as nationally syndicated shows. When a program is not listed with address or phone, just contact the station for more information.

Superstation WTBS
(Turner Broadcasting
System)
1050 Techwood Drive NW
Atlanta, GA 30318-5604
(404) 827-1294

Talk Shows:
Good News
Woman of the 90's

Superstation WWOR
9 Broadcast Plaza
Secaucus, NJ 07096
(201) 330-7440
(201) 330-2488 (FAX)

Talk Shows:
9 Broadcast Plaza
Hispanic Horizon
(201) 330-2101

The Joe Franklin Show
147 West 47th Street
New York, NY 10036
(212) 221-1693

D. Cable Television Network Talk Shows

Following are listings are for major established national cable TV networks, and talk shows. When a particular program is not listed with address or phone, contact the network.

Each of these networks are affiliated with cable television systems with between 20 and 60 million subscribers nationwide. Yet, the number actually watching, is much less and depends on specific ratings. A typical range is 30,000 to 1,000,000 viewers.

Black Entertainment
Network
1899 9th Street NE
Washington, DC 20018
(202) 636-2400

Talk Shows:
BET News
Black Agenda 2000
For The Record

Our Voices
Personal Diary
Teen Summit
Video Soul
This Week in Black
Entertainment

Discovery Channel

Talk Show:
World Monitor Television
Christian Science Monitor
One Norway Street
Boston, MA 02155
(617) 450-7015
(617) 450-2283 (FAX)

ESPN: Entertainment and
Sports Programming
Network
ESPN Plaza
935 Middle Street
Bristol, CT 06010
(203) 585-2000

Talk Show:
Nation's Business Today
BIZNET
1615 H Street NW
Washington, DC 20062
(202) 463-5928

Financial News Network
1251 Avenue of the Americas
New York, NY 10020
(212) 827-0071   N/A

No Listing in NYC

Talk Shows:
Business Tonight

CEO Spotlight
Focus
IRS Tax Beat
Money Talk

Financial News Network
6701 Center Drive West
Los Angeles, CA 90045
(213) 670-1100
(213) 568-2358

not in Service No Current Listing

Talk Shows:
American Entrepreneur
Auto Trends
FNN Newswheel
Inside Corporate America
Shop Talk
Market Wrap

The Art Market Report
AMR Productions, Inc
1500 Broadway #1703
New York, NY 10036
(212) 719-9116
(212) 302-1293 (FAX)

Donoghue Strategies
The Gallatan Corporation
419 Occidental Avenue South,
#600
Seattle, WA 98104
(206) 622-5755

The Insiders with Jack
Anderson
Film Group/UPI Television
2930 Eskridge Road
Fairfax, VA 22031
(703) 204-0183
(703) 207-9862 (FAX)

Lifetime Cable Network
34-12 35th Street
Astoria, NY 11106
(718) 706-3569

Talk Shows:
The Jane Wallace Show
Attitudes
The Great American
   People Poll

Esquire; About Men, For
Women
King Features Entertainment
235 East 45th Street
New York, NY 10017
(212) 455-4380

Physicians' Journal
Update
Lifetime Medical Television
34-12 35th Street
Astoria, NY 11106
(718) 706-3573

Family Practice Update
Lifetime Medical Television
34-12 35th Street
Astoria, New York 11106
(718) 706-3597

CNBC: Consumer News
and Business Channel
2200 Fletcher Avenue
Fort Lee, NJ 07024
(201) 585-2622 *Ask For Viewer Services*
                        N/A
Talk Shows:
America's Vital Signs
Business View
Consumer Speak Out

The Dick Cavett Show
Home and Family
McLaughlin Live
The Money Wheel
Smart Money
The Real Story
Talk Weekend
The Real Estate Report
Money And Emotions
The Media Beat
Your Working Life

C-SPAN
400 North Capitol Street NW
#650
Washington, DC 20001
(202) 737-3220
(202) 737-3323 (FAX)

Talk Shows:
National Call In
Book Notes   *o/o Trahern*
Sara Trahern
Peter Soen

CNN: Cable News Network
1 CNN Center
P O Box 105366
Atlanta, GA 30348-5366
(404) 827-1526

Talk Shows:
Daybreak
Day Watch
Future Watch
Health Week
International Hour
On The Menu
Science & Technology
Week
      (404) 827-1500

Sports Tonight
Travel Guide
World Day

CNN: Cable News Network
5 Penn Plaza, 20th Floor
New York, NY 10001-1878
(212) 714-7800

Talk Shows:
Inside Business _Jenny Harris_
Money Week _Jennifer Rider_
Money Line
Pinnacle
The Style Show With Elsa
    Klensch
Your Money

CNN: Cable News Network
111 Massachusetts Avenue
NW
Washington, DC 20001
(202) 898-7526

Talk Shows:
The Capital Gang

Crossfire
(202) 898-7950
(202) 898-7588 (FAX)

Evans & Novaks
(202) 898-7900

Larry King Live
(202) 898-7984
(202) 898-7617 (FAX)

Newsmaker Saturday
(202) 898-7947
Newsmaker Sunday
(202) 898-7947

CNN: Cable News Network
6430 Sunset Boulevard
Suite 600
Hollywood, CA 90028-7903
(213) 460-5000
(213) 460-5097

Talk Shows:
Showbiz Today
Sonya Live in L.A.

The Nashville Network
2806 Opryland Drive
Nashville, TN 37214-1209
(615) 889-6840
(615) 871-7714 (FAX)

Talk Shows:
Nashville Now

American Magazine
Reidland Productions
2806 Opryland Drive
Nashville, TN 37214-1209
(615) 889-6840
(615) 871-7714 (FAX)

Conversation With Dinah
Fred Tattashore Productions
1717 North Highland #902
Hollywood, CA 90028
(213) 461-8637

Crooke & Chase
Jim Owens Entertainment
1525 McGavock Street
Nashville, TN 37203
(615) 256-7700
(615) 256-7779

**The Family Channel
(Christian Broadcasting
Network)**
CBN Center
Virginia Beach, VA 23468-0001
(804) 424-7777

Talk Shows:
700 Club
Heart to Heart
Scott Ross Straight Talk

E: Canadian Broadcast Television Networks

CTV Television Network
42 Charles Street East
Toronto, Ontario
M4Y1T5, CANADA
416-928-6000

Talk Shows:
Canada AM
Live It Up
Shirley
W-5

**Canadian Broadcasting
Corporation**
P O Box 3223 Station C
Ottawa, Ontario
K1Y1E4, CANADA
613-724-1200

Talk Shows:
Newsday
On The Road Again

F: Canadian Syndicated Talk Show:

City Line
CITY-TV
299 Queen Street West
Toronto, Ontario
M5V2Z5, CANADA
416-591-5757

Databank 2

Television

Talk Show

Stations

A: U.S. Television Talk Show Stations

Following is an ADI Market Rank List of television stations comprised of network-owned-and-operated stations and network affiliate stations in the top 100 markets. Some important independent stations are included in the top markets. These are the stations that are most apt to offer live in-studio interview opportunities for locally produced news and talk shows.

MARKET #1
New York Metro, New York

WABC
7 Lincoln Square
New York, NY 10023
(212) 456-7777

WCBS
524 W 57th Street
New York, NY 10019
(212) 975-4321

WNBC
30 Rockefeller Plaza
New York, NY 10020
(212) 664-4444

WNYW (FOX)
205 E 67th Street
New York, NY 10021
(212) 452-5555

WPIX (Independent)
11 WPIX Plaza
New York, NY 10017
(212) 949-1100

WWOR (Independent)
9 Broadcast Plaza
Secaucus, NJ 07094
(201) 348-0009
(see superstations)

MARKET #2
Los Angeles, California

KABC
4151 Prospect Avenue
Los Angeles, CA 90027
(213) 557-4326
(213) 557-5036 (FAX)

KCBS
6121 Sunset Blvd
Los Angeles, CA 90028
(213) 460-3000

KNBC
3000 W. Alameda Ave.
Burbank, CA 91523
(818) 840-8444
(818) 840-3535 (FAX)

KCAL (Independent)
5515 Melrose Avenue
Los Angeles, CA 90038
(213) 467-9999
(213) 460-6265 (FAX)

KCOP (Independent)
915 N. La Brea Avenue
Los Angeles, CA 90038
(213) 851-1000

KTLA (Independent)
Box 500
5800 Sunset Blvd
Los Angeles, CA 90078
(213) 460-5500
(213) 460-5952 (FAX)
(see superstations)

KTTV (FOX)
5746 Sunset Blvd
Los Angeles, CA 90028
(213) 856-1000

MARKET #3
Chicago, Illinois

WBBM (CBS)
630 N McClurg Court
Chicago, IL 60611
(312) 944-6000

WLS (ABC)
190 N State Street
Chicago, IL 60601
(312) 750-7777

WMAQ (NBC)
NBC Tower
454 N Columbus Drive
Chicago, IL 60611
(312) 836-5555

WGN (Independent)
2501 Bradley Place
Chicago, IL 60618
(312) 528-2311
(see Superstations)

WFLD (Independent)
205 N. Michigan Avenue
Chicago, IL 60601
(312) 565-5532
(312) 565-0420 (FAX)

MARKET #4
Philadelphia,
Pennsylvania

WPVI (ABC)
4100 City Line Avenue
Philadelphia, PA 19131
(215) 878-9700

WCAU (CBS)
City Ave & Monument Road
Philadelphia, PA 19131
(215) 668-5510

KYW (NBC)
Independence Mall E
Philadelphia, PA 19106
(215) 238-4700
WPHL (Independent)
5001 Wynnefield Avenue
Philadelphia, PA 19131
(215) 878-1700

MARKET #5
San Francisco, California

KGO (ABC)
900 Front Street
San Francisco, CA 94111
(415) 954-7777

KPIX (CBS)
855 Battery Street
San Francisco, CA 94111
(415) 362-5550

KRON (NBC)
Box 3412
San Francisco, CA 94119
(415) 441-4444

KTVU (FOX)
Box 22222
Oakland, CA 94623
(415) 834-1212

MARKET #6
Boston, Massachusetts

WCVB (ABC)
5 TV Place
Needham, MA 02192
(617) 449-0400
(617) 449-6682 (FAX)

WNEV (CBS)
7 Bulfinch Pl
Government Center
Boston, MA
(617) 725-0777

WBZ (NBC)
1170 Soldiers Field Road
Boston, MA 02134
(617) 787-7000

WFXT (FOX)
100 Second Avenue
Needham Heights, MA 02194
(617) 449-2525
(617) 455-8768 (FAX)

WSBK (Independent)
83 Leo Birmingham Parkway
Boston, MA 02135
(617) 783-3838

MARKET #7
Detroit, Michigan

WXYZ (ABC)
Box 789
Southfield, MI 48037
(313) 827-7777

WJBK (CBS)
Box 2000
Southfield, MI 48037
(313) 557-2000
(313) 557-1199 (FAX)

WDIV (NBC)
550 W. Lafayette Blvd
Detroit, MI 48231
(313) 222-0444
(313) 222-0471 (FAX)

WKBD (FOX)
Box 50
Southfield, MI 48037-0050
(313) 350-5050
(313) 358-0977

MARKET #8
Dallas-Ft. Worth, Texas

WFAA (ABC)
Communications Center
606 Young Street
Dallas, TX 75202
(214) 748-9631

KXAS (NBC)
Box 1780
3900 Barnett
Ft. Worth, TX 76101
(817) 535-5600

WDFW (CBS)
400 N Griffin
Dallas, TX 75202
(214) 720-4444

KDAF (FOX)
8001 Carpenter Freeway
Dallas, TX 75247
(214) 634-8833
(214) 634-0435 (FAX)

MARKET #9
Washington, DC

WJLA (ABC)
3007 Tilden St NW
Washington, DC 20008
(202) 364-7777

WUSA (CBS)
4001 Brandywine St NW
Washington, DC 20016
(202) 364-3900

WRC (NBC)
4001 Nebraska Avenue NW
Washington, DC 20016
(202) 885-4000

WTTG (FOX)
5151 Wisconsin Ave NW
Washington, DC 20016
(202) 244-5151
(202) 244-1745 (FAX)

MARKET #10
Houston, Texas

KTRK (ABC)
3310 Bissonnet
Houston, TX 77005
(713) 666 0713

KHOU (CBS)
Box 11
Houston, TX 77001-0011
(713) 526-1111
(713) 521-4326 (FAX)

KPRC (NBC)
Box 2222
Houston, TX 77252
(713) 771-4631

KRIV (FOX)
Box 22810
3935 Westheimer Road
Houston, TX 77227
(713) 626-2610

MARKET #11
Cleveland, Ohio

WEWS (ABC)
3001 Euclid Avenue
Cleveland, OH 44115
(216) 431-5555

WJW (CBS)
5800 S Marginal Road
Cleveland, OH 44103
(216) 431-8888

WKYC (NBC)
1403 E 6th Street
Cleveland, OH 44114
(216) 344-3333
(216) 344-3326 (FAX)

MARKET #12
Atlanta, Georgia

WSB (ABC)
1601 W Peachtree St NE
Atlanta, GA 30309
(404) 897-7000

WAGA (CBS)
Box 4207
Atlanta, GA 30302
(404) 875-5551
(404) 898-0238

WXIA (NBC)
1611 W Peachtree St NE
Atlanta, GA 30309
(404) 892-1611

WATL (FOX)
One Monroe Place
Atlanta, GA 30324
(404) 881-3600
(404) 881-3635

WTBS (Independent)
1050 Techwood Dr NW
Atlanta, GA 30348-5264
(404) 827-1947
(404) 827-1717 (FAX)
(see Superstations)

MARKET #13
Minneapolis/St. Paul, MN

KSTP (ABC)
3415 University Avenue
St. Paul, MN 55114
(612) 645-5555
(612) 642-4172 (FAX)

WCCO (CBS)
90 South 11th Street
Minneapolis, MN 55403
(612) 339-4444

KARE (NBC)
8811 Olson Memorial Hwy
Minneapolis, MN 55427
(612) 546-1111

KITN (FOX)
7325 Aspen Lane N
Minneapolis, MN 55428
(612) 424-2929

MARKET #14
Seattle, Washington

KOMO (ABC)
100 4th Ave N
Seatle, WA 98109
(206) 443-4000

KIRO (CBS)
Box C 21326
2807 3rd Ave
Seattle, WA 98111-7000
(206) 728-7777

KING - TV (NBC)
333 Dexter Ave N
Seattle, WA 98109
(206) 448-5555

KCPQ (FOX)
Box 98828
4400 Steilacoom Blvd SW
Tacoma, WA 98499
(206) 582-8613

MARKET #15
Miami, Florida

WPLG (ABC)
3900 Biscayne Blvd
Miami, FL 33137
(305) 576-1010
(305) 573-4856 (FAX)

WTVJ (NBC)
316 N Miami Ave
Miami, FL
(305) 789-4300
(305) 789-4273 (FAX)

WCIX (CBS)
8900 NW 18th Tr
Miami, FL 33172
(305) 593-0606

WSVN (FOX)
1401 79th St
Causeway, FL 33141
(305) 751-6692

MARKET #16
Tampa, Florida

WTSP (ABC)
Box 10000
St. Petersburg, FL 33733
(813) 577-1010

WTVT (CBS)
Box 31113
Tampa, FL 33631-3113
(813) 876-1313

WFLA (NBC)
905 E Jackson St
Tampa, FL 33602
(813) 228-8888
(813) 221-5787 (FAX)

WTOG (FOX)
365 105th Tr NE
St. Petersburg, FL 33716
(813) 576-4444
(813) 577-1806

MARKET #17
Pittsburgh, Pennsylvania

WATE (ABC)
400 Ardmore Blvd
Pittsburgh, PA 15221
(412) 242-4300
(412) 242-4758 (FAX)

KDKA (CBS)
1 Gateway Center
Pittsburgh, PA 15222
(412) 392-2200

WPXI (NBC)
Box 1100
11 Television Hill
Pittsburgh, PA 15230
(412) 237-1100

WPGH (FOX)
750 Ivory Ave
Pittsburgh, PA 15214
(412) 931-5300
(412) 931-8029 (FAX)

MARKET #18
St. Louis, Missouri

KTVI (ABC)
5915 Berthold Ave
St. Louis, Mo 63110
(314) 647-2222

KMOV (CBS)
One Memorial Drive
St. Louis, MO 63102
(314) 621-4444
(314) 621-4775 (FAX)

KSDK (NBC)
Television Plaza
1000 Market Street
St. Louis, MO 63101
(314) 421-5055

KDNL (FOX)
1215 Cole Street
St. Louis, MO 63106
(314) 436-3030

MARKET #19
Sacramento, California

KOVR (ABC)
1216 Arden Way
Sacramento, CA 95815
(916) 927-1313
(916) 922-0654 (FAX)

KXTV (CBS)
400 Broadway
Sacramento, CA 95818
(916) 441-2345

KCRA (NBC)
3 Television Circle
Sacramento, CA 95814-0794
(916) 447-7300

MARKET #20
Denver, Colorado

KSUA (ABC)
1089 Bannock Street
Denver, CO 80123
(303) 893-9000
(303) 825-1562 (FAX)

KCNC (NBC)
Box 5012TA
Denver, CO 80217
(303) 861-4444
(303) 830-6380 (FAX)

KMGH (CBS)
123 Speer Blvd
Denver, CO 80217
(303) 8323-7777

KDVR (FOX)
501 Wazee
Denver, CO 80204
(303) 593-3131

MARKET #21
Phoenix, Arizona

KTVK (ABC)
3435 N 16th Street
Phoenix, AZ 85016
(602) 263-3333
(602) 263-3377 (FAX)

KTSP (CBS)
511 W Adams St
Phoenix, AZ 85003
(602) 257-1234
(602) 271-9477 (FAX)

KPNX (NBC)
Box 711
Phoenix, AZ 85001
(602) 257-1212
(602) 258-8618 (FAX)

KNXV (FOX)
4625 S 33rd Pl
Phoenix, AZ 85040
(602) 243-4151
(602) 268-3347 (FAX)

MARKET #22
Baltimore, Maryland

WJZ (ABC)
TV Hill
Baltimore, MD 21211
(301) 466-0013

WBAL (CBS)
3800 Hooper Ave
Baltimore, MD 21211
(301) 467-3000

WMAR (NBC)
6400 York Road
Baltimore, MD 21212
(301) 377-2222

WBFF (FOX)
3500 Parkdale Ave
Baltimore, MD 21211
(301) 462-4500

MARKET #23
San Diego, California

KGTV (ABC)
Box 85347
San Diego, CA 92138
(619) 237-1010

KFMB (CBS)
7677 Engineer Rd
San Diego, CA 92111
(619) 571-8888

KNSD (NBC)
8330 Engineer Road
San Diego, CA 92111
(619) 279-3939
(619) 279-1076 (FAX)

XETV (FOX)
8253 Ronson Road
San Diego, CA 92111
(619) 279-6666
(619) 268-9388 (FAX)

MARKET #24
Hartford, Connecticut

WTNH (ABC)
Box 1859
New Haven, CT 06580
(203) 784-8888

WFSB (CBS)
Broadcast House
3 Constitution Plaza
Hartford, CT 06115
(203) 728-3333

WVIT (NBC)
1422 New Britain Ave
W. Hartford, CT 06110
(203) 521-3030
(203) 521-3110 (FAX)

WTIC (FOX)
One Corporate Center
Hartford, CT 06103
(203) 527-6161

MARKET #25
Indianapolis, Indiana

WRTV (ABC)
1330 N. Meridian St
Indianapolis, IN 46201
(317) 635-9788

WISH (CBS)
Box 7008
1950 N. Meridian St
Indianapolis, IN 46207
(317) 923-8888

WTHR (NBC)
1000 N. Meridian St
Indianapolis, IN 46204
(317) 636-1313

MARKET #26
Orlando, Florida

WFTV (ABC)
Box 999
Orlando, FL 32802
(407) 841-9000

KCPX (CBS)
Box 606000
Orlando, FL 32860
(407) 291-6000

WESH (NBC)
Box 1551
Orlando, FL 32115
(904) 226-2222
(904) 226-2127 (FAX)

WOFL (FOX)
35 Skyline Drive
Lake Mary, FL 32746
(407) 644-3535

MARKET #27
Portland, Oregon

KATU (ABC)
2153 NE Sandy Blvd
Portland, OR 97232
(503) 231-4222

KOIN (CBS)
222 SW Columbia St
Portland, OR 97201
(503) 464-0600
(503) 464-0707 (FAX)

KGW (NBC)
1501 SW Jefferson St
Portland, OR 97201
(503) 226-5000

MARKET #28
Milwaukee, Wisconsin

WISN (ABC)
Box 402
Milwaukee, WI 53201
(414) 342-TV12

WITI (CBS)
9001 N Green Bay Rd
Milwaukee, WI 53217
(414) 355-6666

WTMJ (NBC)
720 E Capitol Dr
Milwaukee, WI 53201
(414) 332-9611

WCGV (FOX)
5445 N 27th St
Milwaukee, WI 53202
(414) 527-2424

MARKET #29
Cincinnati, Ohio

WKRC (ABC)
1906 Highland Avenue
Cincinnati, OH 45230
(513) 763-5500
(513) 651-0704 (FAX)

WCPO (CBS)
500 Central Ave
Cincinnati, OH 45202
(513) 721-9900

WLWT (NBC)
140 W 9th St
Cincinnati, OH 45202
(513) 352-5000

WXIX (FOX)
10490 Taconic Tr
Cincinnati, OH 45215
(513) 772-1919

MARKET #30
Kansas City, Missouri

KMBC (ABC)
1049 Central
Kansas City, MO 64105
(816) 221-9999
(816) 421-4163 (FAX)

KCTV (CBS)
Box 5555
Kansas City, MO 64109
(913) 677-5555
(913) 677-7284 (FAX)

KZKC (NBC)
2111 Television Pl
Kansas City, MO 64126
(816) 254-6262
(816) 254-3571 (FAX)

KSHB (FOX)
4720 Oak Street
Kansas City, MO 64112
(816) 753-4141

MARKET #31
Charlotte, North Carolina

WSOC (ABC)
Box 34665
Charlotte, NC 28234
(704) 335-4999

WBTV (CBS)
One Julian Price Pl
Charlotte, NC 28208
(704) 374-3500

WCNC (NBC)
Box 18665
Charlotte, NC 28218
(704) 536-3636
(704) 536-1891 (FAX)

WCCB (FOX)
One TV Place
Charlotte, NC 28205
(704) 372-1800
(704) 376-3415 (FAX)

MARKET #32
Salt Lake City, Utah

KTVK (ABC)
1760 Fremont Dr
Salt Lake City, UT 84104
(801) 972-1776

KSL (CBS)
Broadcast House
Salt Lake City, UT 84180-5555
(801) 575-5500

KUTV (NBC)
2185 South, 3600 West
Salt Lake City, UT 84119
(801) 973-3000

KSTU (FOX)
5020 W. Amelia Earhart Dr.
Salt Lake City, UT 84116
(801) 532-1300

MARKET #33
Nashville, Tennessee

WKRN (ABC)
441 Murfreesboro Rd
Nashville, TN 37210
(615) 259-2200

WTVF (CBS)
474 James Robertson Parkway
Nashville, TN 37219
(615) 244-5000

WSMV (NBC)
Box 4
Nashville, TN 37202
(615) 749-2244
(615) 749-2364 (FAX)

MARKET #34
Raleigh - Durham, North Carolina

WTVD (ABC)
Box 2009
Durham, NC 27702
(919) 683-1111

WRAL (CBS)
Box 12000
Raleigh, NC 27605
(919) 821-8555

WPTF (NBC)
3012 High Woods Blvd
Raleigh, NC 27604
(919) 876-0674

WLFL (FOX)
1205 Front St
Raleigh, NC 27609
(919) 821-2200

MARKET #35
Columbus, Ohio

WSYX (ABC)
Box 718
1261 Dublin Road
Columbus, OH 43216-0718
(614) 481-6666

WBNS (CBS)
770 Twin Rivers Dr
Columbus, OH 43215
(614) 460-3700

WCMH (NBC)
Box 4
Columbus, OH 43216
(614) 263-4444
(614) 447-9107 (FAX)

MARKET #36
New Orleans, Louisiana

WVUE (ABC)
Box 13847
New Orleans, LA 70185
(504) 486-6161
(504) 486-2776 (FAX)

WWL (CBS)
1024 N Rampart St
New Orleans, LA 70116
(504) 529-4444
(504) 592-1949 (FAX)

WDSU (NBC)
520 Royal St
New Orleans, LA 70130
(504) 527-0666

WNOL (FOX)
1661 Canal Street
New Orleans, LA 70112
(504) 525-3838

MARKET #37
San Antonio, Texas

KSAT (ABC)
Box 2478
San Antonio, TX 78298
(512) 228-1200

KMOL (NBC)
Box 2641
San Antonio, TX 78299
(512) 226-4251

KENS
5400 Fredericksburg Road
San Antonio, TX 78299
(512) 366-5000
(512) 377-0740 (FAX)

MARKET #38
Greenville, South Carolina

WLOS (ABC)
Box 1300
Asheville, NC 28802
(704) 255-0013

WSPA (CBS)
Box 1717
Spartansburg, SC 29304
(803) 576-7777

WYFF (NBC)
505 Rutherford Street
Greenville, SC 29602
(803) 242-4404
(803) 240-5329 (FAX)

MARKET #39
Memphis, Tennessee

WHBQ (ABC)
485 S Highland Ave
Memphis, TN 38111
(901) 320-1313

WREG (CBS)
803 Channel 3 Dr
Memphis, TN 38103
(901) 577-0100
(901) 577-0198 (FAX)

WMC (NBC)
1960 Union Ave
Memphis, TN 38104
(901) 726-0555

MARKET #40
Buffalo, New York

WKBW (ABC)
7 Broadcast Pl
Buffalo, NY 14202
(716) 845-6100

WIVB (CBS)
2077 Elmwood Ave
Buffalo, NY 14207
(716) 874-4410

WGRZ (NBC)
259 Delaware Ave
Buffalo, NY 14202
(716) 856-1414

WNYB (FOX)
699 Hertel Ave
Buffalo, NY 14207
(716) 875-4919

MARKET #41
Grand Rapids, Michigan

WZZM (ABC)
645 Three Mile Rd NW
Grand Rapids, MI 49504
(616) 784-4200

WWMT (CBS)
590 W. Maple Street
Kalamazoo, MI 49008
(616) 388-3333
(616) 388-8322 (FAX)

WOTV (NBC)
Box B
Grand Rapids, MI 49501
(616) 456-8888
(616) 456-9169 (FAX)

MARKET #42
Norfolk, Virginia

WVEC (ABC)
613 Woodis Ave
Norfolk, VA 23510
(804) 625-1313

WTKR (CBS)
Box 2456
Norfolk, VA 23501
(804) 446-1000
(804) 622-1113 (FAX)

WAVY (NBC)
300 WAVY St
Portsmouth, VA 23704
(804) 393-1010
(804) 397-7628 (FAX)

WTVZ
900 Granby St
Norfolk, VA 23510
(804) 622-3333
(804) 623-1541 (FAX)

MARKET #43
Oklahoma City, Oklahoma

KOCO (ABC)
Box 14555
Oklahoma City, OK 73113
(405) 478-3000

KWTV (CBS)
Box 14159
Oklahoma City, OK 73113
(405) 843-6641

KTVY (NBC)
Box 14068
Oklahoma City, OK 73113
(405) 478-1212

KAUT (FOX)
Box 14843
Oklahoma City, OK 73113
(405) 478-4300

MARKET #44
Providence, Rhode Island

WPRI (ABC)
25 Catamore Blvd
E Providence, RI 02914-1203
(401) 438-7200
(401) 434-3761 (FAX)

WLNE (CBS)
430 County Seat
New Bedford, MA 02741
(617) 992-6666
(401) 751-6666 (FAX)

WJAR (NBC)
111 Dorance Street
Providence, RI 02903
(401) 751-5700

WNAC (FOX)
33 Pine Street
Rehoboth, MA 02769
(617) 252-9711
(508) 252-6240 (FAX)

MARKET #45
Harrisburg, Pennsylvania

WHTM (ABC)
Box 5860
3235 Hoffman St
Harrisburg, PA 17110-5860
(717) 236-2727
(717) 232-5272 (FAX)

WHP (CBS)
Box 1507
Harrisburg, PA 17105
(717) 238-2100

WGAL (NBC)
Lincoln Hwy W
Lancaster, PA 17604
(717) 393-5851

WPMT(FOX)
2005 S Queen St
York, PA 17403
(717) 843-0043
(717) 843-9741(FAX)

MARKET #46
Louisville, Kentucky

WLKY (ABC)
Box 6205
1918 Melwood Ave
Louisville, KY 40206
(502) 893-3671
(502) 897-2384 (FAX)

MARKET #47
Albuquerque, New Mexico

KOAT (ABC)
Box 25982
Albuquerque, NM 87125
(505) 884-7777

KGGM (CBS)
Box 1294
Albuquerque, NM 87103
(505) 243-2285

KOB (NBC)
4 Broadcast Plaza SW
Albuquerque, NM 87104
(505) 243-4411
(505) 764-2522 (FAX)

KSGW (Fox)
Box 25200
Albuquerque, NM 87125
(505) 842-1414

MARKET #48
Charleston, West Virginia

WCHS (ABC)
1301 Piedmont Rd.
Charleston, WV 25301
(304) 346-5358

WOWK (CBS)
Box 13
Huntington, WV 25706-0013
(304) 525-7661

WSAZ (NBC)
645 Fifth Ave.
Huntington, WV 25721
(304) 697-4780

WVAH (Fox)
11 Broadcast Pl.
Hurricane, WV 25526
(304) 757-0011
(304) 757-7533 (FZX)

MARKET #49
Birmingham, Alabama

WBRC (ABC)
Box 6
Birmingham, AL 35201
(205) 322-6666

WBMG (CBS)
2075 Golden Crest Drive
Birmingham, AL 35209
(205) 322-4200

WVTM (NBC)
Box 10502
Birmingham, AL 35202
(205) 933-1313

MARKET #50
Greensboro, North Carolina (High Point, Winston-Salem)

WGHP (ABC)
Box HP-8
High Point, NC 27261
(919) 841-8888

WFMY (CBS)
Box TV2
Greensboro, NC 27420
(919) 379-9369

WXII (NBC)
Box 11847
Winston-Salem, NC 27116
(919) 721-9944
(919) 721-9944 x258 (FAX)

WNRW (FOX)
3500 Myer-Lee Dr
Winston-Salem, NC 27101
(919) 722-4545

MARKET #51
Dayton, Ohio

WDTN (ABC)
4595 S Dixie Ave
Dayton, OH 45401
(513) 293-2101
(513) 294-6542 (FAX)

WHIO (CBS)
1414 Wilmington Ave
Dayton, OH 45401
(513) 259-2111
(513) 259-2024 (FAX)

WKEF (NBC)
1731 Soldiers Home Rd
Dayton, OH 45418
(513) 263-2662

WRGT (FOX)
45 Broadcast Pl
Dayton, OH 45408
(513) 263-4500

MARKET #52
Fresno, California

KJEO (CBS)
Box 5455
Fresno, CA 93755
(209) 222-2411

KFSN (ABC)
1777 G Street
Fresno, CA 93706
(209) 442-1170

KSEE (NBC)
Box 24000
Fresno, CA 93779
(209) 454-2424

MARKET #53
Albany, New York

WTEN (ABC)
341 Northern Blvd
Albany, NY 12204
(518) 436-4822
(518) 462-6065 (FAX)

WRGB (CBS)
1400 Balltown Rd
Schenectady, NY 12309
(518) 346-6666

WNYT (NBC)
15 N Pearl Street
Menands, NY 12204
(518) 436-4791
(518) 436-8723 (FAX)

MARKET #54
Wilkes-Barre, Scranton, Pa.

WNEP (ABC)
16 Montage Mountain Road
Moosie, PA 18507
(717) 346-7474
(717) 347-0359 (FAX)

WYOU (CBS)
415 Lackawanna Ave
Scranton, PA 18503
(717) 961-2222

WBRE (NBC)
62 S Franklin St
Wilkes-Barre, PA 18773
(717) 823-2828

WOLF (FOX)
916 Oak Street
Scranton, PA 18508
(717) 347-9653

MARKET #55
Flint, Michigan

WJRT (ABC)
2302 Lapeer Rd
Flint, MI 48502
(313) 233-3130

WEYI (CBS)
2225 W. Willard Rd.
Clio, MI 48420
(517) 755-0525
(313) 687-1000
(313) 687-4925 (FAX)

WNEM (NBC)
Box 531
107 N Franklin St
Saginaw, MI 48606
(517) 755-8191

WSMH (FOX)
2250 Seymour Ave
Cincinnati, OH 45212
(313) 767-8866

MARKET #56
Little Rock, Arkansas

KATV (ABC)
Box 77
401 South Main Street
Little Rock, AR 72201
(501) 372-7777

KTHV (CBS)
Box 269
Little Rock, AR 72203
(501) 376-1111
(501) 376-3719 (FAX)

KARK (NBC)
201 W 3rd St
Little Rock, AR 72203
(501) 376-2481

WFLX (FOX)
4119 W Blue Heron Blvd
West Palm Beach, FL 33404
(407) 845-2929
(407) 863-1238 (FAX)

MARKET #57
Jacksonville, Florida

WJKS (ABC)
Box 1000
9117 Hogan Rd
Jacksonville, FL 32216
(904) 641-1700

WJXT (CBS)
Box 5270
Jacksonville, FL 32207
(904) 399-4000

WTLV (NBC)
Box TV-12
Jacksonville, FL 32231
(904) 352-1212

MARKET #58
West Palm Beach, Florida

WPEC (CBS)
Box 24612
West Palm Beach, FL 33416-
4612
(407) 844-1212

WPTV (NBC)
Box 510
Palm Beach, FL 33480
(407) 655-5455
(407) 655-8947 (FAX)

MARKET #59
Tulsa, Oklahoma

KTUL (ABC)
Box 8
Tulsa, OK 74101
(918) 446-3351

KOTV (CBS)
302 S Frankfort
Tulsa, OK 74120
(918) 582-6666

KJRH (NBC)
3701 S Peoria
Tulsa, OK 75105
(918) 743-2222
(918) 748-1460 (FAX)

MARKET #60
Richmond, Virginia

WXEX (ABC)
Arboretum Pl
Petersburg, VA
(804) 330-8888
(804) 330-8881 (FAX)

WTVR (CBS)
3301 W Broad St
Richmond, VA 23230
(804) 254-3600

WWBT (NBC)
Box 12
Richmond, VA 23201
(804) 233-5461
(804) 230-2793 (FAX)

WRLH (FOX)
1925 Westmoreland St
Richmond, VA 23230
(804) 358-3535
(804) 358-1495 (FAX)

MARKET #61
Mobile, Alabama
(Pensacola, Florida)

WEAR (ABC)
Box 12278
Pensacola, FL 32581
(904) 456-3333
(904) 455-0159 (FAX)

WKRG (CBS)
555 Broadcast Dr
Mobile, AL 36606
(205) 479-5555

WALA (NBC)
Box 1548
Mobile, AL 36633
(205) 434-1073

WPMI (FOX)
764 St. Michael Street
Mobile, AL 36602
(205) 433-1500
(205) 433-3889 (FAX)

MARKET #62
Wichita, Kansas

KAKE (ABC)
Box 10
Wichita, KS 67201
(316) 943-4221

KWCH (CBS)
2815 E 37th St N
Wichita, KS 67219
(316) 838-1212
(316) 838-3524 (FAX)

KSNW (NBC)
Box 333
833 N Main
Wichita, KS 67201
(316) 265-3333
(316) 262-3344 (FAX)

KSAS (FOX)
316 N West St
Wichita, KS 67203
(316) 942-2424

MARKET #63
Toledo, Ohio

WNWO (ABC)
300 S Byrne Rd
Toledo, OH 43615
(419) 535-0024
(419) 535-0202 (FAX)

WTOL (CBS)
Box 715
730 N Summit St
Toledo, OH 43695-0715
(419) 248-1111

WTVG (NBC)
4247 Dorr Street
Toledo, OH 43607
(419) 531-1313

WUPW (FOX)
Four Seagate
Toledo, OH 43604
(419) 244-3600

MARKET #64
Shreveport, Louisiana
(Texarkana, Texas)

KTBS (ABC)
Box 44227
312 E Kings Hwy
Shreveport, LA 71334
(318) 868-3644
(318) 865-1718 (FAX)

KSLA (CBS)
Box 4812
Shreveport, LA 71104
(318) 222-1212
(318) 677-6703 (FAX)

KTAL (NBC)
3150 N Market Street
Texarkana, TX 71007

KMSS (FOX)
Box 30033
Shreveport, LA 71130
(318) 631-5677
(318) 631-4195 (FAX)

MARKET #65
Roanoke (Lynchburg),
Virginia

WSET (ABC)
Box 11588
Lynchburg, VA 24506
(804) 528-1313

WDBJ (CBS)
Box 7
Roanoke, VA 24077
(703) 344-7000

WSLS (NBC)
Box 2161
Roanoke, VA 24009
(703) 981-9110

MARKET #66
Knoxville, Tennessee

WATE (ABC)
Box 2349
1306 NE Broadway
Knoxville, TN 37901
(615) 637-6666

WKXT (CBS)
Box 59088
Knoxville, TN 37950
(615) 689-8000
(615) 689-9047 (FAX)

WBIR (NBC)
1513 Hutchinson Ave
Knoxville, TN 37917
(615) 637-1010

WKCH (FOX)
Box 3809
109 E. Churchwell Avenue
Knoxville, TN 37917
(615) 971-4343
(615) 637-6957 (FAX)

MARKET #67
Syracuse, New York

WIXT (ABC)
Box 9
5904 Bridge St E
Syracuse, NY 13057
(315) 446-4780

WTVH (CBS)
980 James Street
Syracuse, NY 13203
(315) 425-5555

WSTM (NBC)
1030 James Street
Syracuse, NY 13203
(315) 474-5000

WSYT (FOX)
1000 James Street
Syracuse, NY 13203
(315) 472-6800

MARKET #68
Green Bay, Wisconsin

WFRV (ABC)
Box 19055
Green Bay, WI 54307-9055
(414) 437-5411
(414) 437-4576 (FAX)

WBAY (CBS)
115 S Jefferson
Green Bay, WI 54301
(414) 432-3331

WLUK (NBC)
Box 19011
Green Bay, WI 54307-9011
(414) 494-8711

MARKET #69
Des Moines, Iowa

WOI (ABC)
WOI Building
Ames, IA 50011
(515) 294-5555
(515) 294-8503 (FAX)

KCCI (CBS)
Box 10305
888 9th Street
Des Moines, IA 50306
(515) 247-8888
(515) 247-4931 (FAX)

WHO (NBC)
1801 Grand Ave
Des Moines, IA 50308
(515) 242-3500
(515) 242-3797 (FAX)

MARKET #70
Lexington, Kentucky

WTVQ (ABC)
Box 5590
2940 Bryant Road
Lexington, KY 40555
(606) 233-3600

WKYT (CBS)
2851 Winchester Road
Lexington, KY 40509
(606) 299-0411
(606) 299-2494 (FAX)

WLEX (NBC)
Box 1457
Lexington, KY 40591
(606) 255-4404

MARKET #71
Omaha, Nebraska

KETV (ABC)
27th & Douglas Streets
Omaha, NE 68131
(402) 345-7777
(402) 978-8922 (FAX)

KMTV (CBS)
10714 Mockingbird Drive
Omaha, NE 68127
(402) 592-3333

WOWT (NBC)
3501 Farnam Street
Omaha, NE 68131
(402) 346-6666

KPTM (FOX)
4625 Farnam Street
Omaha, NE 68132
(402) 558-4200

MARKET #72
Portland, Maine

WMTW (ABC)
Box 9501 D.T.S.
119 Middle St
Portland, ME 04112-9501
(207) 775-1800
(207) 782-1800

WGME (CBS)
Box 1731
Broadcast Center
Portland, ME 04104
(207) 797-9330

WCSH (NBC)
One Congress Sq
Portland, ME 04101
(207) 772-0181

WPXT (FOX)
2320 Congress St
Portland, ME 04102

MARKET #73
Rochester, New York

WOKR (ABC)
4225 W Henrietta Rd
Rochester, NY 14623
(716) 334-8700

WHEC (NBC)
191 East Ave
Rochester, NY 14604
(716) 546-5670
(716) 454-7433 (FAX)

WROC (CBS)
201 Humboltd St
Rochester, NY 14610
(716) 288-8400

WUHF (FOX)
360 East Ave
Rochester, NY 14604
(716) 232-3700

MARKET #74
Austin, Texas

KVUE (ABC)
Box 9927
Austin, TX 78766
(512) 459-6521
(512) 459-6538 (FAX)

KTBC (CBS)
Box 2223
Austin, TX 78768
(512) 476-7777
(512) 469-0039 (FAX)

KXAN (NBC)
Box 490
Austin, TX 78767
(512) 476-3636

KBVO (FOX)
Drawer 2728
Austin, TX 78768
(512) 835-0042
(512) 837-6753 (FAX)

MARKET #75
Springfield (Champaign,
Decatur), Illinois

WAND (ABC)
904 Southside Dr
Decatur, IL 62521
(217) 424-2500

WICS (NBC)
2680 East Cook St
Springfield, IL 62703
(217) 753-5620

WCIA (CBS)
509 S. Neil
Champaign, IL 61820
(217) 356-8333

MARKET #76
South Bend, Indiana

WSJV (ABC)
58096 CR No. 7 South
Elkhart, IN 46517
(219) 293-8616
(219) 294-1324 (FAX)

WSBT (CBS)
300 W Jefferson Blvd
South Bend, IN 46601
(219) 233-3141

MARKET #77
Paducah, Kentucky
(Harrisburg, Illinois)

WSIL (ABC)
21 Country Aire Road
Harrisburg, IL 62918
(618) 985-2333

WPSD (NBC)
Box 1197
Paducah, KY 42001
(502) 422-8214

MARKET #78
Spokane, Washington

KXLY (ABC)
W 500 Boone Ave
Spokane, WA 99201
(509) 328-9084
(509) 328-5274 (FAX)

KREM (CBS)
Box 8037
S 4103 Regal
Spokane, WA 99223
(509) 448-2000
(509) 838-7308

KHQ
Box 8088
Spokane, WA 99203
(509) 448-6000

KAYU
Box 8115
Spokane, WA 99203
(509) 448-2828
(509) 448-3815 (FAX)

MARKET #79
Bristol (Kingsport, Johnson City), Tennessee

WKPT (ABC)
Box WKPT
Kingsport, TN
(615) 246-9578

WJHL (CBS)
Box 1130
Johnson City, TN 37601
(615) 926-2151

MARKET #80
Columbia, South Carolina

WOLO (ABC)
Box 4217
5807 Shakespeare Road
Columbia, SC 29240
(803) 754-7525
(803) 754-6147 (FAX)

WLTX (CBS)
Drawer M
Columbia, SC 29250
(803) 776-3600

WIS (NBC)
1111 Bull St
Columbia, SC 29201
(803) 799-1010

WACH (FOX)
1221 Sunset Blvd
W Columbia, SC 29169
(803) 791-5757

MARKET #81
Davenport, Iowa (Rock Island, Moline, Illinois)

WQAD (ABC)
3003 Park 16th St
Moline, IL 61265
(309) 764-8888

WHBF (CBS)
231 18th St
Rock Island, IL 61201
(309) 786-5441
(309) 788-4975 (FAX)

KWQC (NBC)
805 Brady St
Davenport, IA 52803
(319) 383-7000
(319) 383-7165 (FAX)

KLJB (FOX)
937 E 53rd St
Suite D
Davenport, IA 52807
(319) 386-1818

MARKET #82
Jackson, Mississippi

WAPT (ABC)
Box 10297
Jackson, MS 39209
(601) 922-1607
(601) 922-1663 (FAX)

WJTV (CBS)
Box 8887
Jackson, MS 39284
(601) 372-6311

WLBT (NBC)
715 S Jefferson Street
Jackson, MS 39205
(601) 948-3333

WDBD (FOX)
Box 10888
7440 Ch 16 Way
Jackson, MS 39289
(601) 922-1234
(601) 922-6752 (FAX)

MARKET # 83
Chattanooga, Tennessee

WTVC (ABC)
Box 1150
Chattanooga, TN 37401
(615) 756-5500

WDEF (CBS)
3300 Broad St
Chattanooga, TN 37408
(615) 267-3392

WRCB (NBC)
900 Whitehall Road
Chattanooga, TN 37405
(615) 267-5412

WDSI (FOX)
2401 E Main St
Chattanooga, TN 37404
(615) 697-0661
(615) 697-0650 (FAX)

MARKET #84
Cedar Rapids, Iowa

KCRG (ABC)
Box 816
Second Ave At 5th St SE
Cedar Rapids, IA 52401
(319) 398-8422

KGAN (CBS)
Box 3131
Cedar Rapids, IA 52406
(319) 395-9060
(319) 395-0987 (FAX)

KWWL
500 E Fourth
Waterloo, IA 50703
(319) 291-1200

KOCR (FOX)
605 Boysen Rd NE
Cedar Rapids, IA 52402
(319) 378-1028

MARKET #85
Springfield, Missouri
KSPR (ABC)
1359 St. Louis St.
Springfield, MO 65802
(417) 831-1333

KOLR (CBS)
Box 1716
Springfield, MO 65801
(417) 862-1010

KYTV (NBC)
Box 3500
Springfield, MO 65808
(417) 868-3800
(417) 868-3894 (FAX)

KDEB (FOX)
3000 Cherry Street
Springfield, MO 65804
(417) 862-2727

MARKET # 86
Tucson, Arizona

KGUN (ABC)
Box 5707
Tucson, AZ 85703
(602) 792-9933

KOLD (CBS)
115 W. Drachman St.
Tucson, AZ 85705
(602) 624-2511

KVOA (NBC)
Box 5188
Tucson, AZ 85703
(602) 792-2270

MARKET #87
Huntsville, Alabama

WAAY (ABC)
1000 Monte Sano Blvd
Huntsville, AL 35801
(205) 533-3131
(205) 533-6616 (FAX)

WHNT (CBS)
960 Monte Sano Blvd
Huntsville, AL
(205) 539-1919

WAFF (NBC)
Box 2116
Huntsville, AL 35804
(205) 533-4848

MARKET #88
Johnstown (Altoona),
Pennsylvania

WATM (ABC)
1450 Scalp Ave
Johnstown, PA 15904
(814) 266-8088

WTAJ (CBS)
Commerce Park
Altoona, PA 16603
(814) 944-2031
(814) 946-8746

WJAC (NBC)
Hickory Lane
Johnstown, PA 15905
(814) 255-7600

MARKET #89
El Paso, Texas

KVIA (ABC)
4140 Rio Bravo
El Paso, TX 79902
(915) 532-7777

KDBC (CBS)
Box 1799
El Paso, TX 79999
(915) 532-6551
(915) 544-2591 (FAX)

KTSM (NBC)
801 N Oregon St
El Paso, TX 79902
(915) 532-5421

KCIK (FOX)
3100 N Stanton St
El Paso, TX 79902
(915) 533-1414

MARKET #90
Baton Rouge, Louisiana

WBRZ (ABC)
1650 Highland Rd
Baton Rouge, LA 70802
(504) 387-2222
(504) 336-2246 (FAX)

WAFB (CBS)
Box 2671
Baton Rouge, LA 70821
(504) 383-9999

WVLA
5220 Essen Lane
Baton Rouge, LA 70809
(504) 766-3233
(504) 766-2996 (FAX)

MARKET #91
Youngstown, Ohio

WYTY (ABC)
3800 Shady Run Lane
Youngstown, OH 44502
(216) 783-2930

WKBN (CBS)
3930 Sunset Blvd.
Youngstown, OH 44501
(216) 782-1144
(216) 782-3504 (FAX)

WFMJ (NBC)
101 W Boardman St
Youngstown, OH 44503
(216) 744-8611

MARKET #92
Madison, Wisconsin

WISC (CBS)
7025 Raymond Road
Madison, WI 53719
(608) 271-4321

WKOW (ABC)
Box 100
Madison, WI 53701
(608) 274-1234
(608) 274-9514 (FAX)

WMTV (NBC)
615 Forward Drive
Madison, WI 53711
(608) 274-1515

WMSN (FOX)
7847 Big Sky Drive
Madison, WI 53719
(608) 833-0047
(608) 833-5055 (FAX)

MARKET #93
McAllen-Brownsville,
Texas

KRGV (ABC)
Box 5
Weslaco, TX 78596
(512) 968-5555

KGBT (CBS)
Box 2567
Harlingen, TX
(512) 421-4444

KVEO (NBC)
394 N Expressway
Brownsville, TX 78521
(512) 544-2323

MARKET #94
Evansville, Indiana

WTVW (ABC)
Box 7
477 Carpenter St
Evansville, IN 47701
(812) 422-1121
(812) 465-4365 (FAX)

WEHT (CBS)
Box 25
Evansville, IN 47701
(812) 424-9215

WFIE (NBC)
1115 Mt. Auburn Road
Evansville, IN 47712
(812) 426-1414

WEVV (FOX)
629 Walnut Street
Evansville, IN 47708
(812) 464-4444

MARKET #95
Greenville, North Carolina

WCTI (ABC)
Box 2325
Newbern, NC 28561
(919) 638-1212
(919) 637-4141 (FAX)

WNCT (CBS)
Box 898
Greenville, NC 27835-0898
(919) 756-3180
(919) 756-5381 (FAX)

WITN (NBC)
Box 468
Washington, NC 27889
(919) 946-3131

MARKET #96
Waco (Temple, Bryan),
Texas

KXXV (ABC)
Box 2522
Waco, TX 76702
(817) 754-2525

KWTX (CBS)
Box 2636
6700 American Pl
Waco, TX 76712
(817) 776-1330
(817) 751-1088 (FAX)

KCEN (NBC)
Box 188
Temple, TX 76503
(817) 773-6868

KWKT (FOX)
Box 2544
Waco, TX 76702-2544
(817) 776-3844

MARKET #97
Las Vegas, Nevada

KTNV (ABC)
3355 Valley View Blvd
Las Vegas, NV 89102
(702) 876-1313

KLAS (CBS)
Box 15047
Las Vegas, NV 89114
(702) 733-8850
(702) 734-7437 (FAX)

KVBC (NBC)
1500 Foremaster Lane
Las Vegas, NV 89101
(702) 642-3333

KVVU
25 TV 5 Drive
Henderson, NV 89014
(702) 435-5555

MARKET #98
Springfield, Massachusetts

WGGB (ABC)
Box 40
1300 Liberty Street
Springfield, MA 01102-0040
(413) 733-4040

WWLP (NBC)
Box 2210
Springfield, MA 01102
(413) 786-2200

MARKET #99
Savannah, Georgia

WJCL (ABC)
Box 13646
Savannah, GA
(912) 925-0022

WTOC
Box 8086
Savannah, GA 31412
(912) 234-1111

WSAV (NBC)
Box 2429
Savannah, GA 31402
(912) 651-0300

MARKET #100
Burlington, Vermont
(Plattsburgh, New York)

WCAX (CBS)
Box 608
Burlington, VT 05402
(802) 658-6300

WVNY (ABC)
Box 22
100 Market Sq
Burlington, VT 05401
(802) 658-8022

WPTZ (NBC)
Old Moffitt Road
North Pole, NY 12901
(518) 561-5555

B: Canadian Television Talk Show Stations

The following is a list of Canadian major-market television stations, affiliated with networks. These are the stations that are most apt to offer interviews on locally produced talk shows.

ALBERTA

CBRT (CBC)
Box 2640
1724 Westmount
Calgary T2P 2M7
Alberta, Canada
403-283-8361

CBXFT (CBC)
Box 555
Edmonton T5J 2P4
Alberta, Canada
403-468-7500

BRITISH COLUMBIA

CJDC (CBC)
901 102nd Avenue
Dawson Creek V1G 2B6
British Columbia, Canada
604-782-3341

CBUT (CBC)
Box 4600
Vancouver, V6B 4A2
British Columbia, Canada
604-662-6000

CHAN (CTV)
Box 4700
Vancouver V6B 4A3
British Columbia, Canada
604-420-2288
604-421-9427 (FAX)

ONTARIO

CBOFT (CBC)
Box 3220
STN C
250 Lanark
Ottowa, K1Y 1E4
Ontario, Canada
613-724-5233

CJOH (CTV)
Box 5813
STN F
Ottowa, K2C 3G6
Ontario, Canada
(613) 224-1313

CBLT (CBC)
Box 500 Terminal A
354 Jarvis St
Toronto, M5W 1E6
Ontario, Canada
416-925-3311

CFTO (CTV)
Box 9
Toronto M4A 2M9
Ontario, Canada
416-963-8980

QUEBEC

CFCF (CTV)
405 Ogilvy Avenue
Montreal, H3N 1M4
Quebec, Canada
514-273-6311

CBVT (CBC)
Box 10400
Quebec City, G1V 2X2
Quebec, Canada
418-654-1341
418-654-3207 (FAX)

SASKATCHEWAN

CBKST (CBC)
5th Floor
CN Tower
Saskatoon S7K 1J5
Saskatchewan, Canada
306-244-1911
306-664-1915 (FAX)

CFQC (CTV)
216 First Avenue N
Saskatoon, S7K 3W3
Saskatchewan, Canada
306-665-8600

Databank 3

Radio

Talk Shows

A: Radio Network Programs

Following is a listing of talk-formatted radio programs found on broadcast radio networks. In the case that a particular program is not listed with an address or telephone number, you can contact the network for information.

ABC Radio Network/ABC News/ ABC Information Radio Network
125 West End Avenue
New York, NY 10023-6345
(212) 887-5100

Talk Shows:
Young Adult Newscall
Today's People
Consumer Directions
    (1 minute segments)
Perspective
    (general interest)
Sally Jessy Raphael Show
Speaking of Everything
    (general interest)

American Radio Network
1130 E. Cold Spring Lane
Baltimore, MD 21239
(301) 532-2563
(301) 323-8538 (FAX)

Talk Shows:
Gary Null Show (nutrition)
Paul Bicknell Morning Show (general interest)
Allen Fields Show (lifestyles)
Linda Scott Travel Show
Tom D'Antoni Show (humor-talk)
Dr. Bob Show (health)
Ed Ellison Show (political)
Pet Pourri
Living With Diabetes

**Mark Scheinbaum Show
(financial)**
Nuts and Bolts (auto)
**Ted Byrne Show
(general interest)**
Meg Green Show (financial)

**Business Radio Network
(BRN)**
888 Garden of the Gods Road
Colorado Springs, CO 80907
(719) 528-7040
(719) 528-5170 (FAX)

Talk Shows:
New Venture Money Show
**Omniverse (general
interest)** *– No Longer Carried*
The Home Office
**America's Dining and
Travel Guide**
Computing Success
Scams Across America
**Womens Business
Exchange**
**The Grand Opening
(franchising)**
Investing News
Donoghue Strategies
Sales Talk · *Greg Davis*
The Real Estate Ball Game
Wealth Without Risk
Executive Editions *No*
(CEO interviews) *Longer Carried*
Your Own Success
**(see Syndicated Radio
Shows)** *No Longer Carried*

CBS Radio Network
CBS News
524 West 57th Street
New York, NY 10019
(212) 975-8999 *– Modem*
975-4321

Talk Shows:
Healthtalk
**Newsmark (general
interest)**
News Notes
**Today in Business
(4-minute segments)**
**Osgood File (5-minute
general interest** *Charles Osgood*
segments)
**West 57th
(general interest)**

**CBS Radio Stations News
Service**
51 West 52nd Street
New York, NY 10019
(212) 975-6895

Talk Shows:
Report on Medicine
**Correspondent's Notebook
(5-minute segments)**
Your Dollars
**Count Down To Tomorrow
(2-minute segments on
the future)**
**Dateline America
(3-minute Americana
segments)**

Money News Network
1929 South Manchester
Anaheim, CA 92802
(714) 748-4800
(714) 748-4828 (FAX)

Talk Shows:
Vera's Voice
Investors Club of the Air

Mutual Radio Network
1755 S. Jefferson Davis
Highway
Arlington, VA 22202-3587
(703) 685-2000
(703) 685-2145 (FAX)

**National Public Radio
Network**
2025 M Street NW
Washington, DC 20036-3348
(202) 822-2000
(202) 822-2329 (FAX)

Talk Shows:
Weekend Edition
Morning Edition

**NBC TALKNET/Westwood
One Radio Network**
1700 Broadway 19th Floor
New York, NY 10019-5905
(212) 237-2500
(212) 245-2250 (FAX)

Talk Shows:
Bruce Williams Show
    (general interest)

Dr. Harvey Ruben Show
    (health)
The Dolans
    (personal finance)
Bob Madigan Show
    (general interest)
Money Memo
Neil Myer Show
    (general interest)
Dara Wells Show
    (personal finance)
**Nunnsense (one-minute
    general interest)**
**Source Report
    (arts/public affairs)**

Sun Radio Network
2857 Executive Drive
Clearwater, FL 34622
(813) 572-9209
(813) 572-4735 (FAX)

Talk Shows:
**Weekend Nightlight
    (general interest)**
**Rambling with Ramsey
    (general interest)**
America's Issues (politics)
Talking Pets
**American Lawn Garden
    Reports**
A Seer (psychic)
Issues Forum
Farm Talk
American Outdoors
**For the People
    (consumer advocate)**
**Coffee With Cassie Jacobi
    (national issues)**
National Soapbox

Not with Network

= **Today's Business Journal**
All Sports Magazine
American Dream
   (home repair)
Radio Free America
   (general interest)
Real Estate Action Line
Psychic Astrologer

UPI Radio Network
Five Penn Plaza
New York, NY 10001
(212) 560-1190

Talk Show:
Feature File
   (2-minute segments,
   general interest)

UPI Radio Network
(United Press
International)
316 West 2nd Street
6th Floor
Los Angeles, CA 90012-3504
(213) 620-0977
(213) 620-1237 (FAX)

Talk Show:
Reflection/View From The
   West

USA Radio Network
P O Box 1000
Carrollton, TX 75011
(214) 484-3900
(214) 243-3489 (FAX)

Talk Show:
Youth Talk USA
In Touch Networks, Inc.
322 West 48th Street
New York, NY 10036
(212) 586-5588
Access (general interest)
Open Forum (blind and
   reading-impaired service)

National Black Network
41-30 58th Street
Woodside, NY 11377
(718) 565-5757

Talk Shows:
Action Woman
Black Issues And The
Black Press
Black Viewpoint
   (2 1/2-minute features)
Night Talk (black issues)

Daynet
c/o ABC Radio
125 West End Avenue
Sixth Floor
New York, NY 10023
(212) 787-2110 _ Private Number
212 · 613 - 3800
212 - 955 · 9222
Talk Shows
The Dr. Joy Brown Show
The Alan Colmes Show
   (political issues)
The Barry Farber Show

MAJorNet
312 · 755 · 1300
Julia Heath

B: Syndicated Radio Talk Shows

These shows are syndicated to radio stations on a market-by-market basis. Some may appear on a national network as well. Some may require in-person interviews, rather than telephone interviews. Some are short features.

Your Own Success
(The author's show, taped in NYC, also on BRN; motivation, entrepreneur, business)
P O Box 279
Norwood, NJ 07648
(201) 784-0059 _PRIVATE Number_

About Town/Focus
(general interest)
697 West End Avenue #6A
New York, NY 10025-6823
(212) 749-3647

Ray Briem Show/
Michael Jackson Show
(general interest)
KABC-3321 South La Cienega Blvd.
Los Angeles, CA 90016-3114
(213) 840-4963
(213) 837-1955 (FAX)

Bookworm - KCRW
(general interest - books)
1900 Pico Blvd.
Santa Monica, CA 90405
(213) 450-5183

Americans At Their Best
Narwood Productions
40 East 49th Street
New York, NY 100178-1110
(212) 755-3320

Radio America
906 Glaize Wood Court
Tacoma Park, MD 20912-5836
(301) 270-0598

Talk Shows:
Mrs. Sharp's Traditions
(children)
Kaleidoscope (humanities,
entertainment)

Something You Should
Know (lifestyle)
Strand Broadcast Services
1461 9th Street
Manhattan Beach, CA 90266
(213) 372-6282

The Sound of Travel
Studio M Productions
8715 Waikiki Station
Honolulu, HI 96830-0715
(808) 734-3345
(808) 734-3299

Fresh Air
(general interest)
WHYY-FM
150 North 6th Street
Philadelphia, PA 19106-1589
(215) 351-1281

**Moody Broadcasting
Network**
820 No. La Salle
Chicago, IL 60610
(312) 329-4300

Talk Shows:
Morning Clock (family)
Close Up (family)
Prime Time (family)
Open Line (family)

AMEX Business Talk
The American Stock Exchange
86 Trinity Place
New York, NY 10006
(212) 306-1637   Tom Manium

**Carol Lynley Radio
Program/**
**Joan Fontaine Radio
Program/**
(5-min. general interest spots)
Rowland Industries, Inc.
P O Box 941
Teaneck, NJ 07666
(201) 833-0501
Casper Citron
(general interest)
350 Central Park West
New York, NY 10025
(212) 222-3333

In Touch With Your Health
Associated Radio Reading
Service
322 West 48th Street
New York, NY 10036
(212) 586-5588

**Lou Adler's Medical
Journal/**
New Perspectives
(3-minute & 2-minute
segments)
P O Box 430
North Salem, NY 10560
(914) 669-5277

Present Tense
(general interest)
Cinema Sound, LTD.
165 E. 56th Street
New York, NY 10022
(212) 751-4000

Real Estate Action Line
888 Seventh Avenue
New York, NY 10019
(212) 586-5700

**Richard Roffman And
Friends/News Desk**
(15-minute segments each)
Roffman Productions
697 West End Avenue
New York, NY 10025
(212) 749-3647

Dow Jones Report
one-minute business/finance
segments)
Dow Jones & Company
New York, NY 10281
(212) 416-2116

Voice of America
(airs daily-24 hours in foreign
countries)
26 Federal Plaza
New York, Ny 10278
(212) 264-2345

Databank 4

Radio

Talk Show

Stations

A. Radio Stations in Top 100 Markets

The following is a rank market-by-market list of radio stations that are known to program or offer talk shows as part of their programming. The list includes the top 100 (ADI) markets. ADI is a designation meaning "area of dominant influence."

These top 100 ADI markets represent more than 80 percent of the American population. There are a total of 209 ADI markets. (The remaining 109 are listed by city rank at the conclusion of the list.)

Important Note: Most of these stations offer telephone interviews

MARKET #1
New York Metropolitan area

WABC - AM
2 Penn Plaza
17th Floor
New York, NY 10021
(212) 613-3836
(212) 947-1340 (FAX)

Call individual shows

WBAI - FM
505 8th Avenue
19th Floor
New York, NY 10018-6587
(212) 599-2141 — *Private Number*
(212) 599-3226 (FAX)

WLIB - FM
801 Second Avenue
2nd Floor
New York, NY 10017-4761
(212) 953-0300 · Disconnected

WCTC - AM / WMGQ - FM
P O Box 100
New Brunswick, NJ 08901-0100
908 (201) 249-2600 Call individual
908 (201) 249-9010 (FAX) Shows

WERA - AM
120 West 7th Street
Plainfield, NJ 07060-1682
(201) 696-1300 Private #
(201) 241-0449 (FAX)

MVOX - AM / WRTN - FM
One Broadcast Forum
New Rochelle, NY 10801-2094
(914) 636-1460 Call individual
(914) 636-2900 (FAX) Shows

WCBS - FM
51 West 52nd Street
New York, NY 10019-6188
(212) 975-4321 Call individual
(212) 975-9123 Shows

WOR - AM
1440 Broadway
New York, NY 10018-2301
(212) 391-2800 On the Air Line

WNYC - AM
One Center Street
New York, NY 10007-2316
(212) 669-7800 Disconnected
(212) 669-8986 Disconnected

WWRL - AM
41-30 58th Street
Woodside, NY 11377 Call individual Shows
(718) 335-1600

WFAS - AM/FM
P O Box 551
White Plains, NY 10602-0551 Call individual Shows
(914) 693-2400
(914) 693-4489 (FAX)

MARKET #2
Los Angeles, California
KFI - AM
610 South Ardmore
P O Box 76860
Los Angeles, CA 90076-0860
(213) 385-0101

KIEV - AM
505 So. Flower Street
Los Angeles, CA 90071-2185
(818) 246-1135
(213) 245-5438 (FAX)

KBIG - FM
7755 Sunset Boulevard
Los Angeles, CA 90046-3998
(213) 874-7700
(213) 874-4276 (FAX)

KALI - AM
5723 Melrose Avenue
Hollywood, CA 90038
(213) 466-6161

KQLZ - FM
6430 Sunset Blvd, #1102
Hollywood, CA 90028-7914
(213) 469-1631
(213) 856-4698 (FAX)

KIIS- AM/FM
6255 Sunset Blvd
Hollywood, CA 90028-7403
(213) 466-8381
(213) 466-9030 (FAX)

KNX - AM / KODJ - FM
6121 Sunset Blvd.
Los Angeles, CA 90028-6493
(213) 460-3657
(213) 463-9270

KLOS - FM
3321 S. La Cienega Blvd
Los Angeles, CA 90016-3197
(213) 557-7243

KABC - AM
3321 South La Cienega Blvd
Los Angeles, CA 90016-3114
(213) 840-4901
(213) 837-1955 (FAX)

KRLA - AM / KLSX - FM
3580 Wilshire Blvd
Los Angeles, CA 90010
(213) 383-4222
(213) 386-3649

KACE - FM
3650 W. Martin Luther King
Blvd
Los Angeles, CA 90008
(213) 330-3100
(213) 412-7803 (FAX)

KDAY - AM
1700 North Alvarado Blvd
Los Angeles, CA 90026
(213) 665-1150

MARKET #3
Chicago, Illinois

WGN - AM
435 N. Michigan
Chicago, IL 60611
(312) 222-4700
(312) 222-5165(FAX)

WMBI
820 N. LaSalle
Chicago, IL 60610
(312) 329-4300

WGCI - AM
332 S. Michigan Avenue
Suite 600
Chicago, IL 60604-4804
(312) 427-4800

WBEZ - FM
105 W. Adams Street
39th Floor
Chicago, IL 60603
(312) 890-8225
(312) 641-6234 (FAX)

WJJD - AM
180 N. Michigan Ave
Chicago, IL 60601-7401
(312) 977-1800
(312) 855-1043 (FAX)

MARKET #4
Philadelphia,
Pennsylvania

WCAU - AM
City Line & Monument Road
Philadelphia, PA 19131-1195
(215) 668-5800
(215) 668-5540 (FAX)

WUSL - FM
440 Domino Lane
Philadelphia, PA 19128-4399
(215) 483-8900
(215) 483-5930 (FAX)

WIP - AM
441 N. Fifth Street
Philadelphia, PA 19123
(215) 922-5000
(215) 922-2364 (FAX)

WHYY - FM
150 N. 6th Street
Philadelphia, PA 19106-1589
(215) 351-1281

WXPN - AM
3905 Spruce Street
Philadelphia, PA 19104
(215) 898-6677

MARKET #5
San Francisco, California

KGO - AM
900 Front Street
San Francisco, CA 94111-1450
(415) 954-7777

KFRC - AM
500 Washington Street
San Francisco, CA 94111-2968
(415) 986-6100
(415) 951-2329 (FAX)

KCBS - AM / KRQR - FM
One Embarcadero Center, #3200
San Francisco, CA 94111
(415) 765-4050
(415) 765-4080

KNBR - AM
1700 Montgomery St. #400
San Francisco, CA 94111-1071
(415) 951-7093
(415) 951-7024

MARKET #6
Boston, Massachusetts

WODS - FM
30 Winter Street
Boston, MA 02108
(617) 426-2200
(617) 728-1958 (FAX)

WHDH - AM
7 Bulfinch Street
Boston, MA 02114-5019
(617) 725-0777
(617) 742-8827 (FAX)

WBZ - AM
1170 Soldier's Field Road
Boston, MA 02134-1004
(617) 787-7000
(617) 783-0213 (FAX)

WMBR - FM
3 Ames Street
Cambridge, MA 02142-1305
(617) 494-8810

WRKO - AM
3 Fenway Plaza
Boston, MA 02215-2597
(617) 236-6800
(617) 236-6886 (FAX)

WBCN - FM
1265 Boylston Street
Boston, MA 02215-3410
(617) 266-1111

MARKET #7
Detroit, Michigan

WJR Radio
2100 Fisher Building
Detroit, MI 48202
(313) 875-4440
(313) 875-8141 (FAX)

WNIC - FM
15001 Michigan Avenue
Dearborn, MI 48126-2963
(313) 846-8500
(313) 846-1068 (FAX)

WAAM - AM
4230 Packard Road
Ann Arbor, MI 48108
(313) 971-1600
(313) 973-2916 (FAX)

WXYT - AM
15600 West 12 Mile Road
South Field, MI 48076-3068
(313) 569-8000
(313) 569-9866

WCSX - FM / WHND - AM
One Radio Plaza
Detroit, MI 48220-2140
(313) 398-7600
(313) 542-0313 (FAX)

WDTR - FM
9345 Lawton Avenue
Detroit, MI 48206
(313) 494-1570

MARKET #8
Dallas, Texas

KVTT - FM
P O Box 30
Dallas,TX 75221
(214) 484-2020
(214) 243-3489 (FAX)

KLIF - AM
3500 Maple Avenue #1600
Dallas, TX 75219-3901
(214) 526-2400
(214) 520-4343 (FAX)

KVIL - AM/FM
5307 East Mockingbird #500
Dallas, TX 75206-5109
(214) 826-7900
(214) 826-8105 (FAX)

KDBN - AM
5956 Sherry Lane
Dallas, TX 75225
(214) 691-1075

MARKET #9
Washington, DC

WPGC - AM
P O Box 10239
Washington, DC 20018
(301) 441-3500

WTOP - AM
3400 Idaho Avenue NW
Washington, DC 20016
(202) 895-5000
(202) 895-5077 (FAX)

WAMU - FM
The American University
Washington, DC 20016
(202) 885-1030

WMAL - AM / WRQX - FM
4400 Jennifer Street NW
Washington, DC 20015-2113
(202) 686-3100

WPFW - FM
702 H Street NW
Washington, DC 20001
(202) 783-3100
(202) 783-3106 (FAX)

MARKET #10
Houston, Texas

KPRC - AM
8181 S.W. Freeway
P O Box 2222
Houston, TX 77252-2222
(713) 771-4631
(713) 995-8334 (FAX)

KTRH - AM
P O Box 1520
Houston, TX 77251
(713) 526-5874
(713) 630-3666 (FAX)

KIKK - AM/FM
6306 Gulfton Drive
Houston, TX 77081-1195
(713) 772-4433
(713) 995-7956 (FAX)

KILT - AM/FM
500 Lovett Blvd
Houston, TX 77006-4099
(713) 526-3461
(713) 526-5458 (FAX)

KUHF - FM
4600 Gulf Freeway
#500
Houston, TX 77004
(713) 749-7186
(713) 748-1212 (FAX)

MARKET #11
Cleveland, Ohio

WHK - AM
Statler Office Tower
1127 Euclid Avenue
Cleveland, OH 44115
(216) 781-1420

WBBG - AM
3940 Euclid Avenue
Cleveland, OH 44115-2506
(212) 391-1260
(216) 391-1814 (FAX)

WJMO - AM / WRQC - FM
2156 Lee Road
Cleveland Heights, OH 44118
(216) 371-3534
(216) 371-0174 (FAX)

WERE - AM
1500 Chester Avenue
Cleveland, OH 44114-3615
(216) 696-1300
(216) 241-0449

WTGR - FM
2156 Lee Road
Cleveland Heights, OH
44118-2908
(216) 371-3534
(216) 371-0174

WLTF - FM / WRMR - AM
One Radio Lane
Cleveland, OH 44114-4016
(216) 696-4444
(216) 781-5143 (FAX)

WWWE - AM
1250 Superior Avenue
Cleveland, OH 44114-3236
(216) 781-1100
(216) 566-0764 (FAX)

MARKET #12
Atlanta, Georgia

WAEC - AM
1465 Northside Drive #14
Atlanta, GA 30318
(404) 355-8600

WSB - AM
1601 W. Peachtree Street N.E.
Atlanta, GA 30309-2433
(404) 897-7540
(404) 897-7525 (FAX)

WGST - AM
550 Pharr Road NE
#400
Atlanta, GA 30305-3431
(404) 233-0640
(404) 237-5856 (FAX)

WAPW - FM
3405 Piedmount Road, #500
Atlanta, GA 30305
(404) 266-0997
(404) 266-0166 (FAX)

WALR - FM
209 CNN Center
Atlanta, GA 30303
(404) 688-0068

MARKET #13
Minneapolis (St. Paul),
Minn.

KUOM - AM
330 - 21st Avenue S
Minneapolis, MN 55454
(612) 625-3500

KQRS - AM/FM
917 N Lilac Drive
Minneapolis, MN 55422-4688
(612) 545-5601
(612) 593-3040 (FAX)

KYCK - AM
5730 Duluth Street
Golden Valley, MN 55422
(612) 544-3196
(612) 544-0519

KDWB - AM/FM
708 South 3rd Street, #200
Minneapolis, MN 55415
(612) 340-9000
(612) 340-9560

WCCO - AM
625 Second Avenue S
Minneapolis, MN 55402-1912
(612) 370-0611
(612) 370-0683 (FAX)

KSTP - AM
2792 Maplewood Drive
Maplewood, MN 55109-1017
(612) 481-9333
(612) 481-9324 (FAX)

WDGY - AM
611 Frontenac Place
St. Paul, MN 55104
(612) 645-7757
(612) 642-5223 (FAX)

MARKET #14
Seattle, Washington

KUOW - FM
University of Washington
Seattle, WA 98195-0001
(206) 543-2710

KJR - AM
190 Queen Ave N
P O Box 3726
Seattle, WA 98124-3726
(206) 285-2295
(206) 286-2376 (FAX)

KIRO - AM
2807 Third Avenue
Seattle, WA 98121-1260
(206) 728-7777
(206) 441-7905 (FAX)

KING - AM
333 Dexter Avenue N
Seattle, WA 98109-5183
(206) 448-3666
(206) 448-0928 (FAX)

KISW - FM
712 Aurora Ave N
Seattle, WA 98109-4314
(206) 258-7625
(206) 282-7018 (FAX)

KEZX - AM
3876 Bridge Way N
Seattle, WA 98103
(206) 633-5590

MARKET #15
Miami, Florida

WNWS - AM
20450 NW 2nd Avenue
Miami, FL 33169-2505
(305) 653-8811
(305) 652-5385 (FAX)

WIOD - AM
1401 N. Bay Causeway
Miami, FL 33141-4104
(305) 759-4311
(305) 757-7516 (FAX)

WHQT - FM
3200 Ponce de Leon Blvd.
Coral Gables, FL 33134
(305) 445-5411
(305) 446-8477 (FAX)

WINZ - AM
4330 NW 207 Drive
Miami, FL 33055-1250
(305) 624-6101
(305) 621-4954

WSBR - AM
5700 N. Federal Highway
Boca Raton, FL 33487
(407) 997-0074

MARKET #16
Tampa (St. Petersburg), Fla.

WFLA - AM
801 Jackson Street
Tampa, FL 33602
(813) 839-9393
(813) 831-3299 (FAX)

WTKN - AM
11300 4th Street N
#318
St. Petersburg, FL 33716
(813) 223-7419
(813) 578-2477 (FAX)

MARKET #17
Pittsburgh, Pennsylvania

WDUQ - FM
Duquesne University
Pittsburgh, PA 15282-0001
(412) 434-6401
(412) 434-6294 (FAX)

WDKA - AM
Gateway Center
Pittsburgh, PA 15222
(412) 392-2000

WEEP - AM
107 6th Street
Fulton Building
Pittsburgh, PA 15222
(412) 471-9950

WTAE - AM
400 Ardmore Blvd
Pittsburgh, PA 15221
(412) 731-1250
(412) 244-4596 (FAX)

WDVE - FM
200 Fleet Street
Pittsburgh, PA 15220
(412) 226-4664
(412) 937-1207 (FAX)

MARKET #18
St. Louis, Missouri

KMOX - AM / KLOU - FM
1 Memorial Drive
St. Louis, MO 63102-2498
(314) 621-2345
(314) 444-3230 (FAX)

KATZ - AM
1139 Olive Street #303
Saint Louis, MO 63101-1994
(314) 241-6000
(314) 241-7498 (FAX)

KSLH - FM
1517 S. Teresa
St. Louis, MO 63104
(314) 865-4550

WCEO - AM
7711 Carondelet
Suite 304
St. Louis, MO 63105-3385
(618) 259-0059

KFUO - AM
85 Founders Lane
Clayton, MO 63105
(314) 725-3030
(314) 725-3801 (FAX)

KLOU - FM / KMOX - AM
1 Memorial Drive
St. Louis, MO 63102-2498
(314) 621-2345
(314) 444-3230 (FAX)

KMJM - FM
532 Debaliviere
St. Louis, MO 63112
(314) 361-1108

KATZ - AM
1139 Olive Street #303
St. Louis, MO 63101-1994
(314) 241-6000
(314) 241-7498 (FAX)

MARKET #19
Sacramento, California

KZAP - AM
P O Box 15985
Sacramento, CA 95852-1985
(916) 925-3700

KRXQ - FM
5301 Madison Avenue
#402
Sacramento, CA 95841
(916) 334-7777

KCTC - FM
2225 19th Street
Sacramento, CA 95818
(916) 441-5282
(916) 446-4142 (FAX)

KXOA - AM \ KQPT - FM
280 Commerce Circle
Box 1677
Sacramento, CA 95808
(916) 923-6840

MARKET #20
Denver, Colorado

KOA - AM \ KRFX - FM
1380 Lawrence St #1300
Denver, CO 80204
(303) 893-8500
(303) 825-0337 (FAX)

KHOW - AM
8975 E. Kenyon Avenue
Denver, CO 80237-1897
(303) 694-6300

KBPI - FM
1 Tabor Center
17th Street #2300
Denver, CO 80202-5823
(303) 572-6200
(303) 572-6210 (FAX)

MARKET #21
Phoenix, Arizona

KOY - AM/FM
840 N. Central Avenue
Phoenix, AZ 85004
(602) 258-8181
(602) 420-9912 (FAX)

KFYI - AM
631 N. First Avenue
Phoenix, AZ 85003
(602) 258-6161
(602) 252-9563 (FAX)

KFNN - AM
65 E. First Avenue
Mesa, AZ 85210
(602) 644-1510
(602) 644-1589 (FAX)

KTAR - AM
301 W. Osborn Road
Phoenix, AZ 85013-3921
(602) 274-6200
(602) 266-3858 (FAX)

KXEG - AM
1817 N. Third Street #202
Phoenix, AZ 85004-1586
(602) 254-5333

MARKET #22
Baltimore, Maryland

WEAA - AM
Morgan State University
Cold Spring Lane
Baltimore, MD 21239
(301) 444-3564

WBAL - AM
3800 Hooper Avenue
Baltimore, MD 21211-1397
(301) 467-3000
(301) 338-6483 (FAX)

WIYY - FM
3800 Hooper Avenue
Baltimore, MD 21211-1397
(301) 889-0098
(301) 467-3294 (FAX)

MARKET #23
San Diego, California

KSDO - AM
5050 Murphy Canyon Road
San Diego, CA 92123
(619) 278-1130
(619) 285-4364 (FAX)

KFMB - AM/FM
7677 Engineer Road
San Diego, CA 92111-1582
(619) 571-8888

MARKET #24
Hartford, Connecticut

WPOP - AM
P O Box 11-1410
Hartford, CT 06111-7539
(203) 666-1411
(203) 665-1175 (FAX)

WELI - AM
495 Benham Street
Hamden, CT 06514
(203) 281-9600
(203) 281-7640 (FAX)

MARKET #25
Indianapolis, Indiana

WICR - AM
1400 East Hanna Avenue
Indianapolis, IN 46227
(317) 788-3280
(317) 788 3275 (FAX)

WNDE - AM
6161 Fall Creek Road
Indianapolis, IN 46220
(317) 257-7565
(317) 253-6501 (FAX)

MARKET #26
Orlando, Florida

WONQ
2483 John Young Parkway
Suite R
Orlando, FL 32804
(407) 290-2020

MARKET #27
Portland, Oregon

KBPS - AM/FM
546 N.E. 12th Avenue
Portland, OR 97232-2719
(503) 280-5828

MARKET #28
Milwaukee, Wisconsin

WISN - AM
759 N. 19th Street
Milwaukee, WI 53233-2126
(414) 342-1111
WTMJ - AM
720 E. Capital Drive
PO BOX 620
Milwaukee, WI 53201-0620
(414) 332-9611
(414) 223-5298 (FAX)

WYMS - FM
P O Drawer 10K
Milwaukee, WI 53201
(414) 475-8389

MARKET #29
Cincinnati, Ohio

WKRC - AM
1906 Highland Avenue
Cincinnati, OH 45219-3104
(513) 763-5500
(513) 241-9444 (FAX)

WEBN - FM
2724 Erie Avenue
Cincinnati, OH 45208
(513) 871-8500
(513) 749-3299 (FAX)

WCKY - AM
219 McFarland Street
Cincinnati, OH 45202-2614
(513) 241-6565
(513) 381-8439 (FAX)

WLW - AM
1111 Saint Gregory Street
Cincinnati, OH 45202
(513) 241-9597
(513) 852-1004 (FAX)

WRRM - FM
205 West 4th Street, #1200
Cincinnati, OH 45202
(513) 241-9898
(513) 241-6689 (FAX)

WDJO - AM
225 East Sixth Street
Cincinnati, OH 45202
(513) 621-6960
(513) 621-0789 (FAX)

MARKET #30
Kansas City, Missouri

KCMO - AM
508 Westport Road
Kansas City, MO 64111
(816) 931-2681
(816) 932-7301 (FAX)

KCUR - FM
5100 Rockhill Road
Kansas City, MO 64110
(816) 276-1551
(816) 276-1717 (FAX)

MARKET #31
Charlotte, North Carolina

WBT - AM/FM
1 Julian Price Place
Charlotte, NC 28208-5211
(704) 374-3575

WFAE - FM
University of North Carolina
Charlotte, NC 28223-0001
(704) 597-2555

MARKET #32
Salt Lake City, Utah

KSL - AM
Broadcast House
Salt Lake City, UT 84180-1160
(801) 575-6397

MARKET #33
Nashville, Tennessee

WLAC - AM
10 Music Circle East
Nashville, TN 37203
(615) 256-0555
(615) 242-4826

MARKET #34
Raleigh-Durham, N.C.

WCLY - AM
647 Maywood Avenue
Raleigh, NC 27603
(919) 821-1550

WDNC - AM
Box 2126
Durham, NC 27702
(919) 682-0318

MARKET #35
Columbus, Ohio

WCBE - FM
270 E. State Street
Columbus, OH 43215-4312
(614) 365-5555

WTVN - AM
42 E. Gay Street
Columbus, OH 43215-3119
(614) 224-1271
(614) 365-9203 (FAX)

WOSU - AM
2400 Olentangy River Road
Columbus, OH 43210-1027
(614) 292-9678
(614) 292-0513 (FAX)

MARKET #36
New Orleans, Louisiana

WNOE - AM
529 Bienville
New Orleans, LA 70130
(504) 529-1212

WSMB - AM
629 S. Clairborne Avenue
New Orleans, LA 70113
(504) 566-1350

WTIX - AM
3421 N. Causeway Blvd.
Suite 800
Metairie, LA 70002
(504) 834-9849
(504) 834-9898 (FAX)

WVOG - AM
2730 Lou Mour Avenue
Metairie, LA 70001
(504) 831-6941

WWL - AM
1024 N. Rampart Street
New Orleans, LA 70116
(504) 529-4440

MARKET #37
San Antonio, Texas

WOAI - AM
6222 NW 1-H 10
San Antonio, TX 78201
(512) 734-7301
(512) 735-8811 (FAX)

MARKET #38
Greenville, South Carolina

WFBC - AM
505 Rutherford Street
PO Box 1330
Greenville, SC 29602-1330
(803) 271-9200

WKCN - AM
P O Box 1364
Mount Pleasant, SC 29464
(803) 881-1400

MARKET #39
Memphis, Tennessee

WMC - AM/FM
1960 Union Avenue
Memphis, TN 38104-4031
(901) 726-0477
(901) 272-9186 (FAX)

MARKET #40
Buffalo, New York

WEBR - AM
23 North Street
Buffalo, NY 14202-1190
(716) 886-0970

WGR - FM
464 Franklin Street
Buffalo, NY 14202-1302
(716) 881-4555
(716) 888-9726 (FAX)

WBEN - AM/FM
2077 Elmwood Avenue
Buffalo, NY 14207-1974
(716) 876-1344
(716) 875-6201 (FAX)

WWKB - AM
695 Delaware Avenue
Buffalo, NY 14209
(716) 884-5101
(716) 882-2048 (FAX)

MARKET # 41
Grand Rapids, Michigan

WCSG - FM
1159 E. Beltline Avenue NE
Grand Rapids, MI
49505-5803
(616) 942-1500

MARKET #42
Norfolk (Newport News), Virginia

WNIS - AM
1302 Ingleside Road
Norfolk, VA 23502
(804) 853-8500

WGH - FM
Pembroke One
Virginia Beach, VA 23462
(804) 497-1310

MARKET #43
Oklahoma City, Oklahoma

KTOK - AM
P O Box 1000
Oklahoma City, OK 73101-1000
(405) 840-5271
(405) 840-4025 (FAX)

MARKET #44
Providence, Rhode Island
(New Bedford, MA)

WPRO - AM
1502 Wampanoag Trail
East Providence, RI 02915-1075
(401) 433-4200
(401) 433-5967 (FAX)

WHJJ - AM
115 Eastern Avenue
East Providence, RI 02914
(401) 438-6110
(401) 438-9588 (FAX)

WERI - AM/FM
P O Box 325
Westerly, RI 02891-0325
(401) 596-7728
(401) 596-6688 (FAX)

WADK - AM
140 Thames Street
P O Box 367
Newport, RI 02840-0367
(401) 846-1540
(401) 848-5460 (FAX)

WBSM - AM
220 Union Street
New Bedford, MA 02740-5994
(508) 993-1767

MARKET #45
Harrisburg (Lancaster), Pa.

WHP - AM
Box 1507
Harrisburg, PA 17105
(717) 238-2100

WKBO - AM
2814 Green Street
Harrisburg, PA 17110
(717) 232-1800

WLAN - AM
252 N. Queen Street
Lancaster, PA 17603
(717) 394-7261

WLPA -AM
24 S. Queen Street
Lancaster, PA 17603
(717) 397-0333

MARKET #46
Louisville, Kentucky
WAVG - AM
800 South 4th Street
Louisville, KY 40203
(502) 587-0970
(502) 540-3228

WFPL
York & 4th Streets
Louisville, KY 40203
(502) 561-8640
(502) 561-8657 (FAX)

MARKET #47
Albequerque, New Mexico

KKIM - AM
301 Los Ranchos NW
Albequerque, NM 87107
(505) 898-5185

KMBA - AM
2403 San Mateo NE Suite W-2
Los Ranchos de Albuquerque,
NM 87110
(505) 883-4066

MARKET #48
Charleston, West Virginia

WCAW - AM / WVAF - FM
P O Box 4318
Charleston, WV 25364-4318
(304) 925-4986

WXIT - AM
136 High Street
Charleston, WV 25311
(304) 342-4166

MARKET #49
Birmingham, Alabama

WAPI - AM
2146 Highlands Avenue S
Birmingham, AL 35205
(205) 933-9274
(205) 933-2748 (FAX)

WERC - AM
3700 4th Avenue S
PO Box 10904
Birmingham, AL 35202-0904
(205) 591-7171
(205) 591-6322 (FAX)

MARKET #50
Greensboro, Winston-Salem, North Carolina

WTOB - AM
2400 Warwick Road
Winston-Salem, NC 27104
(919) 759-0363
(919) 759-0366 (FAX)

WSMX - AM
Box 16049
Winston-Salem, NC 27115
(919) 761-1545

MARKET #51
Dayton, Ohio

WHIO - AM
P O Box 1206
Dayton, OH 45420
(513) 259-2111
(513) 944-0475 (FAX)

MARKET #52
Fresno, California

KMJ - AM
P O Box 70002
1110 East Olive
Fresno, CA 93744
(209) 229-5800

MARKET #53
Albany (Schenectady), New York

WQBK -AM
P O Box 1300
Albany, NY 12201-1300
(518) 462-5555
(518) 462-0784 (FAX)

WPYX - FM
1050 WTRY Road
Schenectady, NY 12309-1699
(518) 785-9800

WGY - AM
1430 Balltown Road
Schenectady, NY 12309-4301
(518) 381-4800
(518) 381-4855

MARKET #54
Wilkes-Barre, Pennsylvania

WILK -AM
88 N. Franklin Street
Wilkes-Barre, PA 18711
(717) 825-9898

MARKET #55
Flint (Saginaw), MI

WSGW - AM
1795 Tittabawassee Road
Box 1945
Saginaw, MI 48605
(517) 752-3456
(517) 754-5046 (FAX)

MARKET #56
Little Rock, Arkansas

KARN - AM
4021 W. 8th Street
PO Box 4189
Little Rock, AR 72204-4189
(501) 661-7500
(501) 661-7583 (FAX)

MARKET #57
Jacksonville, Florida

WOKV - AM
6869 Lenox Ave, PO Box 6877
Jacksonville, FL 32236
(904) 783-3711

MARKET #58
West Palm Beach, Florida

WJNO - AM
P O Box 189
West Palm Beach, FL 33402-0189
(305) 838-4300
(305) 838-4357 (FAX)

WPBR - AM
3000 S. Ocean Blvd.
Palm Beach, FL 33480-5698
(407) 582-7401
(407) 582-9254 (FAX)

MARKET #59
Tulsa, Oklahoma

KRMG - AM
7136 S. Yale
Tulsa, OK 74136-6315
(918) 493-7400
(918) 493-2376 (FAX)

KAKC - AM / KMOD - FM
5801 East 41st Street #900
Tulsa, OK 74135-5601
(918) 664-2810
(918) 665-0555 (FAX)

MARKET #60
Richmond, Virginia

WCVE - FM
23 Sesame Street
Richmond, VA 23235
(804) 320-1301

MARKET #61
Mobile, Alabama

WKRG - AM
555 Broadcast Drive
Box 160587
Mobile, AL 36616-1587
(205) 479-5555
(205) 473-8130

MARKET #62
Wichita, Kansas

KXLK - FM
P O Box 1839
626 N. Broadway
Wichita, KS 67201
(316) 267-0807
(316) 267-0512 (FAX)

MARKET #63
Toledo, Ohio

WSPD - AM
125 S.Superior
Toledo, OH 43602
(419) 244-8321
(419) 244-7631 (FAX)

MARKET #64
Shreveport, Louisiana

KEEL - AM
Box 2007
Shreveport, LA 71120
(318) 425-8692

MARKET #65
Roanoke, Virginia

WVTF - FM
4235 Electric Road SW
Roanoke, VA 24014
(703) 857-8900
(703) 857-7578 (FAX)

WFIR - AM / WPVR - FM
Towers Mall
P O Box 150
Roanoke, VA 24002-0150
(703) 345-1511

MARKET #66
Knoxville, Tennessee

WIVK - AM/FM
P O Box 10207
Knoxville, TN 37939-0207
(615) 588-6511
(615) 588-3725 (FAX)

MARKET #67
Syracuse, New York

WSYR - AM
2 Clinton Square
Syracuse, NY 13202-1042
(315) 472-9797

WAER-FM
215 University Place
Syracuse, NY 13244-2100
(315) 423-4046

MARKET #68
Green Bay, Wisconsin
(No Talk Stations Found)

MARKET #69
Des Moines, Iowa

WHO - AM
1801 Grand Avenue
Des Moines, IA 50308-3362
(515) 242-3670
(515) 242-3798 (FAX)

MARKET #70
Lexington, Kentucky

WBKY - FM
University of Kentucky
Lexington, KY 40506-0001
(606) 257-3221

MARKET #71
Omaha, Nebraska

KFAB - AM
5010 Underwood Avenue
Omaha, NE 68132-2297
(402) 556-8000
(402) 556-8937 (FAX)

MARKET #72
Portland, Maine

WGAN - AM
200 High Street
Portland, ME 04101
(207) 774-4561

MARKET #73
Rochester, New York

WXXI - AM
280 State Street
Rochester, NY 14601
(716) 325-7500

MARKET #74
Austin, Texas

KLBJ - AM
8309 1H 35 North
P O Box 1209
Austin, TX 78767
(512) 832-4000
(512) 832-4081 (FAX)

KFIT - AM
9049 Old Jollyville Road #102
Austin, TX 78759
(512) 794-8400

MARKET #75
Springfield (Champaign), Illinois

WDWS - AM
P O Box 677
Champaign, IL 61820-0677
(217) 351-5300
(217) 351-5385 (FAX)

WTAX -AM / WDBR - FM
P O Box 2759
Springfield, IL 62708-2759
(217) 753-5400
(217) 753-7902 (FAX)

MARKET #76
South Bend, Indiana

WAMJ - AM
P O Box 6580
1129 N. Hickory
South Bend, IN 46615-3724
(219) 234-1580

MARKET #77
Paducah, Kentucky
(Cape Girardeau, Missouri)

KZIM - AM
Box 1610
324 Broadway
Cape Girardeau, MO
(314) 335-8291

MARKET #78
Spokane, Washington

KXLY - AM/FM
West 500 Boone Avenue
Spokane, WA 99201-2497
(509) 328-7173
(509) 328-5274 (FAX)

MARKET #79
Bristol, Tennessee

WHCB - FM
Box 2061
Bristol, TN 37621-2061
(615) 878-6279

WOPI - AM
288 Delaney Street
Bristol, TN 37620
(615) 764-5131

MARKET #80
Columbia, South Carolina

WVOC - AM
Box 21567
Columbia, SC 29221
(803) 798-5255

MARKET #81
Davenport, Iowa

WOC - AM
3535 E. Kimberly Road
Davenport, IA 52807
(319) 344-7000

MARKET #82
Jackson, Mississippi

WMAA - FM
Box 4343
Jackson, MS 39216-0343
(601) 982-0500

WMPR - FM
Box 31052
Jackson, MS 39206
(601) 956-0212

MARKET #83
Chattanooga, Tennessee

WDEF - AM
3300 S. Broad Street
Chattanooga, TN 37408
(615) 267-3392
(615) 267-0009 (FAX)

WDOD - AM
Box 4232
Old Baylor School Road
Chattanooga, TN 37405
(615) 266-5117

WGOW - AM
Box 11202
Chattanooga, TN 37401
(615) 756-6141

MARKET #84
Cedar Rapids, Iowa

KHAK - AM/FM
425 Second Street SE
#450
Cedar Rapids, IA 52401
(319) 365-9431

WMT - AM
600 Old Marion Road NE
Cedar Rapids, IA 52406
(319) 395-0530
(319) 393-0918 (FAX)

MARKET #85
Springfield, Missouri

KICK - AM
610 College Street
Springfield, MO 65805
(417) 865-1340

MARKET #86
Tucson, Arizona
KCEE - AM
2100 N. Silverbell Road
Tucson, AZ 85745
(602) 623-7556
(602) 792-1019 (FAX)

KTUC - AM
P O Box 40188
76 S. Stone Avenue
Tucson, AZ 85701-1772
(602) 622-3344

KNST - AM
4400 E Broadway #200
Tucson, AZ 85711
(602) 323-9400
(602) 327-9384 (FAX)

MARKET #87
Huntsville, Alabama

WLRH - FM
University of Alabama
4701 University Drive
Huntsville, AL 35899
(205) 895-9574

MARKET #88
Johnstown, Pennsylvania

WRTA - AM
1417 12th Avenue
P O Box 272
Altoona, PA 16603
(814) 943-6112
(814) 944-9782 (FAX)

MARKET #89
El Paso, Texas

KTSM - AM
801 N. Oregon
El Paso, TX 79902
(915) 532-5421

MARKET #90
Baton Rouge, Louisiana

WJBO - AM
Box 496 - 444 Florida
Baton Rouge, LA 70821
(504) 383-5271
(504) 388-0526 (FAX)

MARKET #91
Youngstown, Ohio

WBBW - AM
418 Knox Street
Youngstown, OH 44502-2218
(216) 744-4421
(216) 744-0720 (FAX)

MARKET #92
Madison, Wisconsin

WHA - FM
Vilas Hall
University of Wisconsin
Madison, WI 53706
(608) 263-3970
(608) 263-9763 (FAX)

WTDY - AM
P O Box 2058
Madison, WI 53701
(608) 271-1484
(608) 281-1329 (FAX)

MARKET #93
McAllen-Brownsville,
Texas
(no talk stations found)

MARKET #94
Evansville, Indiana
(no talk stations found)

MARKET #95
Greenville (Washington),
North Carolina

WRRF - AM
Box 1707
Washington, NC 27889
(919) 946-2162

MARKET #96
Waco (Temple), Texas

WACO - AM
Box 21088
Waco, TX 76702
(817) 772-7100

WTEM - AM
Box 1230
Temple, TX 76503
(817) 773-5252

MARKET # 97
Las Vegas, Nevada

KLAV - AM
364 Convention Center Drive
Las Vegas, NV 89109
(702) 796-1230

KCEP - FM
330 W. Washington St.
Las Vegas, NV 89106
(702) 648-4218

KDWN - AM
One Main Street
Las Vegas, NV 89101-6312
(702) 385-7212
(702) 385-6094 (FAX)

MARKET #98
Springfield, Massachusetts

WSPR - AM
Box 1270
Springfield, MA 01102
(413) 732-4182

MARKET #99
Savannah, Georgia

WCHY - AM
P O Box 1247
Savannah, GA 31402-1247
(912) 964-7794
(912) 964-9414 (FAX)

MARKET #100
Burlington, Vermontt
(Plattsburgh, New York)

WKDR - AM
85A West Canal Street
Winooski, VT 05404
(802) 655-5154
(802) 655-5170 (FAX)

B. ADI Markets 101-209 listed by rank

101. Ft. Wayne, Indiana
102. Charleston, South Carolina
103. Lansing, Michigan
104. Salinas California
105. Colorado Springs, Colo.
106. Lincoln, Nebraska
107. Montgomery, Alabama
108. Sioux Falls, South Dakota
109. Peoria, Illinois
110. Fargo, North Dakota
111. Ft. Meyers, Florida
112. Augusta, Georgia
113. Santa Barbara, California
114. Lafayette, Louisiana
115. Tallahassee, Florida
116. Ft. Smith, Arkansas
117. Corpus Christi, Texas
118. Tyler, Texas
119. Columbus, Georgia
120. Monroe, Arkansas
121. Macon, Georgia
122. Eugene, Oregon
123. Amarillo, Texas
124. Reno, Nevada
125. Yakima, Washington
126. Columbus, Mississippi
127. La Crosse, Wisconsin
128. Bakersfield, California
129. Wausau, Wisconsin
130. Traverse City, Michigan
131. Beaumont, Texas
132. Wichita Falls, Oklahoma
133. Duluth, Minnesota
134. Binghamton, New York
135. Boise, Idaho
136. Florence, South Carolina
137. Terre Haute, Indiana
138. Topeka, Kansas
139. Erie, Pennsylvania
140. Rockford, Illinois
141. Chico, California
142. Sioux City, Iowa

143. Wheeling, Virginia
144. Albany, Georgia
145. Minot, North Dakota
146. Odessa, Texas
147. Wilmington, N. C.
148. Bluefield, West Virginia
149. Lubbock, Texas
150. Rochester, Minnesota
151. Joplin, Missouri
152. Medford, Oregon
153. Columbia, Missouri
154. Clarksburg, West Virginia
155. Bangor, Maine
156. Biloxi, Mississippi
157. Idaho Falls, Idaho
158. Quincy, Missouri
159. Abilene, Texas
160. Dothan, Alabama
161. Utica, New York
162. Alexandria, Louisiana
163. Salisbury, Maryland
164. Greenwood, Mississippi
165. Laurel, Mississippi
166. Rapid City, South Dakota
167. Watertown, New York
168. Elmira, New York
169. Gainesville, Florida
170. Billings, Montana
171. Panama City, Florida
172. Lake Charles, Louisiana
173. El Centro, Arizona
174. Harrisonburg, Virginia
175. Palm Springs, California
176. Jonesboro, Arkansas

177. Missoula, Montana
178. Ardmore, Oklahoma
179. Meridian, Mississippi
180. Grand Junction, Colorado
181. Great Falls, Montana
182. Tuscaloosa, Alabama
183. Marquette, Michigan
184. Jackson, Tennessee
185. Eureka, California
186. San Angelo, Texas
187. Laredo, Texas
188. Bowling Green, Kentucky
189. Butte, Montana
190. Lafayette, Indiana
191. Anniston, Alabama
192. St. Joseph, Missouri
193. Casper, Wyoming
194. Hagerstown, Maryland
195. Lima, Ohio
196. Cheyenne, Wyoming
197. Charlottesville, Virginia
198. Zanesville, Ohio
199. Parkersburg, West Virginia
200. Flagstaff, Arizona
201. Twin Falls, Idaho
202. Presque Isle, Maine
203. Victoria, Texas
204. Ottumwa, Iowa
205. Bend, Oregon
206. Mankato, Minnesota
207. Helena, Montana
208. North Platte, Nebraska
209. Alpena, Michigan

C: Canadian Talk Radio Stations

The following is a market-by-market listing of Canadian talk-formatted radio stations. Important Note: Most of these stations offer telephone interviews.

Alberta:

CJOC - AM
Box 820
Lethridge T1J 3Z9
Alberta Canada
403-320-1220

British Columbia:

CKNW - AM
815 McBride Plaza
V3L 2C1
New Westminster
British Columbia, Canada
604-522-2711

CIGV - FM
125 Nanaimo Ave West
Penticton V2A 1N2
British Columbia, Canada
604-493-6767

CJAV - AM
2970 Third Avenue
Port Alberni V9Y 7N4
British Columbia, Canada
604-723-2455

Saskatchewan:

CFQC - AM
216 First Ave North
Saskatoon S7K 3W3 SK
Saskatchewan, Canada
306-665-8600
306-665-0450 (FAX)

Nova Scotia:

CBI - AM
Box 700
Sydney B1P 6H7
Nova Scotia, Canada
902-539-5050

Ontario:

CFRN - AM
Box 710
Niagara Falls L2E 6X7
Ontario, Canada
416-356-6710
416-356-0696 (FAX)

CBL - AM
Box 500 Station A
Toronto M5W 1E6
Ontario, Canada
416-975-7400

CFRB - AM
2 St. Clair Avenue W
Toronto M4V 1L6
Ontario, Canada

CKWW - AM
300 Cabana Road E
Windsor N9G 1AE
Ontario, Canada
519-966-7000
519-966-1090 (FAX)

Quebec:

CBF - AM
Box 6000
Montreal H3C 3A8
Quebec, Canada
514-285-3211

CKVL - AM
211 Gordon Avenue
Verdun H4G 2R2
Quebec, Canada
514-766-2311

CJRP - AM
4200 Sillery
Quebec G1T 2S2
Quebec, Canada
418-688-1060

CBSI - AM
350 Rue Smith
Suite 30
Sept-lles G4R 3X2
Quebec, Canada
418-968-0720

CFCF - AM
1200 McGill College Avenue
Suite 300
Montreal H3B 4G7
Quebec, Canada
514-874-4040
514-393-4659 (FAX)

Index

On
The Air

1. Should I hire a publicist

Al Parinello

About The Author

Al Parinello has been recognized as the world's leading authority on how individuals and organizations can market themselves through the free use of television and radio.

He is the creator, producer and co-host of *"Your Own Success,"* a nationally syndicated radio program. His experience with the media is vast and varied. Mr. Parinello has served as executive producer for dozens of national commercials and television programs. He has interviewed more than 2,500 guests and has appeared, himself, as a guest on numerous television and radio talk shows. In addition, he has also owned radio stations.

TV Guide called him "one of a new breed of space-age super salesmen." At Warners, he headed up the team that developed and marketed the phenominally successful cable networks, Nickelodeon and The Movie Channel (TMC), both of which he named.

Mr. Parinello, an in-demand professional speaker to associations and organizations, talks about the effective use of the media and other professional and personal success-related topics. He lives in Bergen

County, New Jersey, with his wife, Anita, and daughter, Dana.

For information about Al Parinello's professional speaking and media consulting services, write or call:

American Media Ventures
P.O. Box 279
Norwood, N.J. 07648
(201) 784-0059

Career Press

America's Premiere Publisher of books on:

- Career & Job Search Advice
- Education
- Business "How-To"
- Financial "How-To"
- Study Skills
- Careers in Advertising, Book Publishing, Magazines, Newspapers, Marketing & Sales, Public Relations, Business & Finance, the Travel Industry and much, much more.
- Internships

If you liked this book, please write and tell us!

And if you'd like a copy of our FREE catalog of nearly 100 of the best career books available, please call us (Toll-Free) or write!

THE CAREER PRESS
180 Fifth Ave.,
PO Box 34
Hawthorne, NJ 07507
(Toll-Free) 1-800-CAREER-1 (U. S. only)
201-427-0229
FAX: 201-427-2037